DARKNESS
BETWEEN STARS

ʄ

About the Authors

John F. Deane was born in 1943 on Achill Island, Co Mayo. He is the author of two novels and thirteen collections of poems, most recently *Snow Falling on Chestnut Hill: New and Selected Poems* (2012), *Semibreve* (2015), *Dear Pilgrims* (2018) and *Naming of the Bones* (2021), all from Carcanet Press. He is also the author of a memoir, *Give Dust a Tongue* (Columba, 2015). He was President of the European Academy of Poetry and was made Chevalier en l'ordre des arts et des lettres by the French Government. In 1979, he founded Poetry Ireland, the national poetry organization, and *Poetry Ireland Review*. He is a member of Aosdána, and divides his time between Dublin and Leitrim.

James Harpur was born in 1956 in England and studied Classics and English at Trinity College, University of Cambridge. He is the author of six volumes of poetry, most recently *The White Silhouette* (Carcanet Press, 2018) and *The Oratory of Light* (Wild Goose, 2021), the latter inspired by St Columba and St Iona, as well as a translation of Boethius' poetry and a work of non-fiction on Christian mysticism. He has taught English on Crete, worked as a lexicographer and now concentrates solely on poetry. He is a member of Aosdána, and lives near Clonakilty, West Cork.

DARKNESS
BETWEEN STARS

Poems in Search of God

JOHN F. DEANE
&
JAMES HARPUR

THE IRISH PAGES PRESS
2022

Darkness Between Stars
is first published in hardback
on 15 July 2022.

The Irish Pages Press
129 Ormeau Road
Belfast BT7 1SH
Ireland

www.irishpages.org

Typeset in 12/15 pt Monotype Perpetua
Designed and composed by RV, Belfast. Printed by Bell & Bain, Glasgow.

A CIP catalogue record for this book
is available from The British Library.

Dust-jacket photographs of the authors:
Moya Nolan and Dino Ignani.

Cover image of the icon:
Christ the Redeemer, Andrei Rublev, Tretyakov Gallery

ISBN: 978-1-8382018-5-2

This book has been generously funded by the Arts Council of Ireland.

CONTENTS

JAMES HARPUR

INTRODUCTION

We – John F. and James – have known each other for many years and shared readings, discussions, and introduced each other's work, finding friendship and mutual encouragement in discovering that we were both fascinated not only by the life of poetry but also by the divine, the sacred, "God". For a while we have toyed with the idea of putting together a joint selection of our poems, partly to celebrate our shared interests, and partly to see how our different backgrounds might have differentiated our poetic imaginations and metaphysical visions. The result is this volume. Here you will find poems about places – from Achill and Palestine to America and West Cork – saints and mystics, the Christian mysteries, works of music and art (including Rembrandt and Rublev), elegies to the dead, and poems of faith and doubt; all in all, in summary, these are poems in search of God – by which we mean an ultimate reality existing beyond this temporal sphere. In addition to the poems, at the back of the book, we have included an informal email exchange we had in 2018 that explores some of the themes embedded in the poetry.

W.B. Yeats said that the argument with ourselves is the seedbed of poetry; he might have added that poetry also springs from our argument with God, or the absence of God. In contemporary times – brought into sharp focus by the 2020 Covid pandemic – the search for meaning, for certainties, for making sense of our lives and the universe around us has never been greater. We hope that these poems bear witness to our own probings into the ineffable.

John F. Deane & James Harpur

JOHN F. DEANE

PENANCE

They leave their shoes, like signatures, below;
above, their God is waiting. Slowly they rise
along the mountainside where rains and winds go
hissing, slithering across. They are hauling up

the bits and pieces of their lives, infractions
of the petty laws, the little trespasses and
sad transgressions. But this bulked mountain
is not disturbed by their passing, by this mere

trafficking of shale, shifting of its smaller stones.
When they come down, feet blistered and sins
fretted away, their guilt remains and that black
mountain stands against darkness above them.

FRANCIS OF ASSISI 1182 : 1982

Summer has settled in again: ships,
softened to clouds, hang on the horizon;
buttercups, like bubbles, float
on fields of a silver-grey haze; and words
recur, such as light, the sea, and God

the frenzy of crowds jostling towards the sun
contains silence, as eyes contain
blindness; we say, may the Lord
turning his face towards you
give you peace

morning and afternoon the cars moved out
onto the beach and clustered, shimmering,
as silver herring do in a raised net; this
is a raucous canticle to the sun

altissimu, omnipotente, bon Signore

to set up flesh
in images of snow and of white
roses, to preach to the sea
on silence, to man
on love, is to strain towards death
as towards a body without flaw

our poems, too, are gestures of a faith
that words of an undying love
may not be without some substance

words hovered like larks above his head, dropped
like blood from his ruptured hands

tue so'le laude, et onne benedictione

we play, like children, awed and hesitant
at the ocean's edge;
between dusk and dark the sea
as if it were God's long and reaching fingers
appropriates each footprint from the sand

I write down words, such as light, the sea, and God
and a bell rides out across the fields
like a man on a horse with helmet and lance
gesturing foolishly towards night

laudato si, Signore, per sora nostra
morte corporale

at night, the cars project
ballets of brightness and shadow on the trees
and pass, pursuing
darkness at the end of their tunnels of light

the restful voices have been swept by time
beyond that storybook night sky
where silence
drowns them out totally

CHRIST, WITH URBAN FOX

I

He was always there for our obeisance,
simple, ridiculous,
not sly, not fox, up-front – whatever
man-God, God-man, Christ – but there.
Dreadlocks almost, and girlish, a beard
trim in fashion, his feminine
fingers pointing to a perfect
heart chained round with thorns;
his closed and slim-fine lips
inveigling us towards pain.

II

Did he know his future? while his blood
slicked hotly down the timbers did he know
the great hasped rock of the tomb
would open easily as a book of poems
breathing the words out? If he knew
then his affliction is charade, as is our hope;
if he was ignorant – his mind, like ours,
vibrating with upset – then his embrace of pain
is foolishness beyond thought, and there –
where we follow, clutching to the texts –
rests our trust, silent, wide-eyed, appalled.

III

I heard my child scream out
in pain on her hospital bed,
her eyes towards me where I stood
clenched in my distress;

starched sheets, night-lights, night-fevers,
soft wistful cries of pain,
long tunnel corridors down which flesh
lies livid against the bone.

IV

Look at him now, this king of beasts, grown
secretive before our bully-boy modernity,
master-shadow among night-shadows,
skulking through our wastes. I watched a fox
being tossed under car wheels, thrown like dust
and rising out of dust, howling in its agony;
this is not praise, it is obedience,
the way the moon suffers its existence,
the sky its seasons. Man-God, God-man, Christ,
suburban scavenger – he has danced
the awful dance, the blood-jig, has been strung
up as warning to us all, his snout
nudging still at the roots of intellect.

OFFICIUM

Spare me Lord for my days burn off like dew.
What is man that you should magnify him;
why do you tender towards him your heart of love?
You visit him at dawn, touching him with dreams,
whisper to him at dusk, while the swings still shift
and soft rain falls on the abandoned frames.
Why have you made him contrary to you
that he learn baseness, anger and defeat
swallowing his own saliva in sudden dread?
Can you erase his sins, like chalk-marks,
or place your angels as a fence about him?
The trees dreep softly, the attendants are gone home.
Today I will lie down in sand, and if tomorrow
you come in search of me, I am no more.

CANTICLE

Sometimes when you walk down to the red gate
hearing the scrape-music of your shoes across gravel,
a yellow moon will lift over the hill;
you swing the gate shut and lean on the topmost bar
as if something has been accomplished in the world;
a night wind mistles through the poplar leaves
and all the noise of the universe stills
to an oboe hum, the given note of a perfect
music; there is a vast sky wholly dedicated
to the stars and you know, with certainty,
that all the dead are out, up there, in one
holiday flotilla, and that they celebrate
the fact of a red gate and a yellow moon
that tunes their instruments with you to the symphony.

THE STUDY

Over the deal table a flower-patterned oil-cloth;
the boy
has his Bible history open before him; its pictures

of deserts, and of stylised heroes of God's militias;
he is chewing on a pencil-end
as if hunger for knowledge frustrates him and he spits

small splinters out onto the stone-flagged floor;
outside
hydrangeas are in bloom, their sky-blue flowers

big as willow-pattern plates; on the kitchen wall
a picture of Jesus, stylised,
fingers long as tapers, ringlets honey-brown, and eyes

lifted querulously towards the ceiling;
a red, eternal light
flickers weakly below the picture;

but the saddened eyes have lowered, and peer
down on the restless
stooped-over boy, in anger or in mute and trenchant

pleading;
and only a summer bee
distraught against the window, makes any sound.

SLIEVEMORE:
THE ABANDONED VILLAGE

You park your car on a low slope
   under the graveyard wall. Always
there is a mound of fresh-turned earth, flowers
   in pottery vases. There is light, from the sea and the wide

western sky, the Atlantic's
   soft-shoe nonchalance, whistle
of kestrels from the lifting mists, furze-scents, ferns,
      shiverings –
   till suddenly you are aware

you have come from an inland drift of dailiness to this shock
   of island, the hugeness of its beauty
dismaying you again to consciousness. Here
   is the wind-swept, ravenous

mountainside of grief; this is the long tilted valley
      where famine
came like an old and infamous flood
from the afflicting hand of God. Beyond all
   understanding. Inarticulate. And pleading.

Deserted. Of all but the wall-stones and grasses,
   humped field-rocks and lazy-beds; what was commerce
      and family
become passive and inert, space
   for the study of the metaphysics of humanness. You climb

grudgingly, aware of the gnawing hungers,
    how the light leans affably, the way an urchin once might
        have watched
from a doorway;
    you are no more than a dust-mote on the mountainside,

allowing God his spaces; you are
    watercress and sorrel, one with the praying of villagers,
one with their silence, your hands
    clenched in overcoat pockets, standing between one world

and another. It has been easier to kneel
    among the artefacts in the island graveyard, this harnessing
        of craft
to contain our griefs;
    here, among these wind-swept, ravenous acres

where we abandon our acceptably deceased to the
        mountain earth.
    In grace. In trustfulness.
This, too, the afflicting hand of God. Beyond all
    understanding. Inarticulate. Though in praise.

KANE'S LANE

The substance of the being of Jesus
sifts through the substance of mine; I
am God, and son of God, and man. Times I feel

my very bones become so light I may
lift unnoticed above Woods's Wood and soar
in an ecstasy of being over Acres' Lake; times again

I am so dugged, so dragged, my flesh
falls granite while a fluid near congealed
settles on my heart. The Christ – frozen in flight

on the high-flung frame of his cross
leaves me raddled in the grossest of mercies
and I walk the length of Kane's Lane, on that ridge

of grass and cress and plantain
battening down the centre, I sex my tongue
on the flesh juices of blackberries, cinch my jaws on the chalk

bitterness of sloes, certain and unsettled,
lost and found in my body, sifted through a strait and
serpentine love-lane stretched between dawn and night.

WORDS OF THE
UNKNOWN SOLDIER

He stumped us, this Jesus of yours, with his
walking on water, fandango, entrechat, glissade;
birthing, imagine! in a dark cave, out of all knowing; then

he walked the hard-baked earth of Palestine, but not
as you walk, or as I, for behind him the healing flowers grew,
the rosebay willowherb, chamomile, the John's Wort;

we noted, too, that he could walk through walls,
appearing suddenly in the midst of folk as if
he were always there, waiting that they might notice him;

oh yes, this too, he walked on air
leaving them gawping upwards as he rose
higher and higher, like a skylark, walking

into the invisible. That was later. But humankind
will not be cheated of its prey for we claimed him, hailing
him fast to a tree, that he could not move

on water, earth or air, and we buried him in the underearth.
Where, it is said, he took to walking once again,
singing his larksong to the startled, to the stumped, dead.

SHOEMAKER

He sat, cross-legged, on a deal table
as if dropped, ready-made, from an old myth;
sat, all hours, all days, lips pursed and fingers
deft and fast, like the poet

who could see the world through a needle's eye,
difficult though penetrable, a shifting, leathery mass
that might be shaped to something
beautiful, and lasting. Like the itinerant Christ

walking the ranges of Galilee, nowhere to lay down
his head. When I conjugate
Christ, and longing, what I mean
is the lake behind the cobbler's house, its waters

soothing us constantly across the night;
I mean trees, those summer mornings,
standing high and stilled within their being; on wilder days
the winds make shapes amongst them,

ghosts visiting the house, composing
their wind-leaf harmonies: I want to be able to say, again,
Christ. Our island shoemaker sat,
sometimes, outside, half-concentrating, half-

watching people go the road; he was one
in a guild with swallows and the blooming of the haw,
one with the people who went measuring their steps
in to the small chapel to divine their living, who watched

snow falling, visible through the stained-glass windows, flakes
that could be birds migrating, butterflies, or spirits
out on spirit escapades. When I write
cobbler, last or nail, or when I scribble

wine, or bread, or music, what I am stitching for
is Christ, is how love still may permeate
the rush of trucks along the motorways, spray
rising against the windscreens, the wipers sighing.

SNOW FALLING ON CHESTNUT HILL

Denn alles Fleisch es ist wie Gras ... (Brahms)

It is late now in the day; that curving lane
with grass and plantain, clovers and pimpernels
forming a hump along the centre, seems
to be straightening towards a conclusion. I have arrived

in a strange city, evening; (I am hearing
Brahms, the German Requiem, *Selig sind* ... blessed
are they who mourn.)
Boston. A big house, and daunting.

They have warned me of arctic chill
reaching this way, over Canada, the lakes, Chicago;
Herr, lehre doch mich ... I have heard already
oboe-moans through the eldering house, thin

reed-sounds through unseen interstices: O Lord
make me aware of my last end.
The hollow spaces of the house
are stirred along their dust: All flesh, the music tells,

is grass. I listened, dozing gently, silence
encompassing, engaging me;
at the front door I heard ...
(no matter, it is no matter). I stood

watching first snow-flakes
visible against the street-lamps; there was the feel
as of the breathing on my face of a lover, as of the brush
of a kiss, sheer

arctic salt, a hosting. *Wir haben hier*
keine bleibende Statt ...
All flesh
is snow. And snow

does not abide. *Selig sind die Toten*, blessed
are the dead; they are at rest
in the Lord's hands. I slept
fitfully; strange

land, strange house, strange dreams; time
raddling me. I could hear
the sound of the deepest night
lying still under a delicate coming down of snow.

*

I have been wondering
about our blizzards of pain and agony – Lupus, for instance,
immune systems down and civil war along the blood.
Prance of the alpha wolf. Bone

scaffolding showing through.
I lay, restless; my temporary home
whispered to itself in house-language, its wooden shifts
of consonants, its groaning vowels, when there came
          (Christ!)

a sudden rapping
against the door. I listened. Again,
rapping, urgent. I crept down. Opened,
I had to, street door, screen-door. Saw

darkness active out there, snow
swirling, a shape that
formed and faded out of the skirl of white and grey ...
And she came, breathless,

shaking snow from her hair and face, stomping her feet,
stood in the non-light of the hallway and snow
pooled about her shoes. She, dressed in white,
reached to drop – "a gift," she said – one

bright Christmas rose, helleborus,
white-petalled, dark-green-leaved,
across the hallstand.
"You!" I whispered. "You?"

She smiled.
"But we laid you down decades ago," I said, "to rest."
"Isn't it good," she said,
"to hear the crunch, under your feet, of fresh snow?"

"You are. . . in body, then?" "Soul
and body, body and soul. No longer flawed.
I passed where snow is a swarm of whitest butterflies
though I had been growing old with the wolves."

"And why? Why now? And how. . .?"
"I bring," she answered, "gifts. Wolves, too, wolves"
 she whispered, "wolves are the lambs of God."
"Our child," I tried, "is wrapped up tight in pain, God's ways ..."

(I saw, then, the wolf-pack, *canis lupus*, settling under trees, they
lie easy in the snow, you can hear their howl-songs, clarinet-calls
off-key in the moon-enlightened night, drawn-out off-melodies,
lauds chanted to the blood, their green-lit white-shaded eyes
sweeping across the heavens; *canis lupus*, grey-grizzled ancients
of days, the black, the white, the gorgeous fur and in the distance
I heard the freight-train howl of human hungers, a tailed-off
threatening horn-call across the night; wolf-pelt, winter-pelt,
the scars, the tissues, and always snow falling down the everyvein
of air)

"Be peacefilled now," she said, softly as a brushing-by of snow,
"it is late, my traveller, live at peace in the rush
 of arctic wind. We are all
 sunlight, dimmed, all snowfall, thawed."

"Our child. . ."
But she was already moving towards the door, her head
shaking; "All flesh is snow,
 snow-fox, snow-pelt I have been, with you,

 a lover, singing against the moon,
 a lamb ..." The door ... I felt the touch of pre-dawn frost,
 heard snow in its soft slide, its fistfuls from the trees,
"Wolves, too," she said, "wolves

are the lambs of God".
"Wait!" I called, and reached
for her. But she was gone,
suddenly, and there was nothing, "I have

questions ... prayers ..."

Silence, only, and absence. I heard still
the breathing of the snow, a car somewhere
climbing a hill. I stood in darkness. Stood. Perplexed,

as always. A snow-plough passed, the steel blades scraping
against the roads. Soon
cars, roof-racked with snow, would shift
like herds of caribou

down the long parkway. The first
faint light of a new day
touched the window. I saw,
on the hallstand, fresh and beautiful,

one hellebore, one Christmas rose.
I closed my eyes against the dawn and heard
Brahms again: *Wie lieblich sind die Wohnungen* ...
how beautiful your dwellings, Lord, how beautiful :

SEMIBREVE

I sat, in the island chapel, moor's edge, winter;
winds groaned and chistled round the walls outside,
the timbers creaked in the afterwarmth,

ghosts from the quenching slipped up through the rafters;
there was a souring emptiness though I sat entranced
by sacrament and my own minuscule being – when the walls

whispered – *Listen!* There was no-one. There was nothing.
Even the winds had died. And the chill winterlight
had dimmed. But a tiny chime had happened, vibrated

on my inner listening. The tiniest hint of spittle
tipped against my brow but there was nothing when I wiped
my hand across it. The door moaned again, a sudden breeze

forcing it and I stood, watchful, and shaken. That
was the first semibreve sounded of a gifted music.
I am day and night now, listening. Tuned for it, and waiting.

VIOLA D'AMORE

I had been playing Bach on the great organ –
"A mighty fortress is our God" –
the church below me empty in the nowhere afternoon,
bombarde, clarion, celeste

and when I lifted fingers from the keys
it was, for a moment, eternity, and the walls of the world
contained nothing but the lingering breadth of the harmony,

rafters of the loft had lifted while the whole sky
trembled in a breeze that rippled slow across it
till all I knew was the touch of the fingers of Jesus

soft on my fingertips, my body
consciously drawing breath, my bones
refusing their earthy weight, and my soul
ringing with immortality.

PIPE ORGAN

From the organ console, the mirror
showed the empty church below, and my face
animated; I played, for myself alone,
Gelobet seist du, Jesu Christ,

and moved with some élan over manuals and pedalboard,
my body given over to a dance of faith: viol
da gamba – trembling strings, bourdon – the breathfulness
of the flute; and for a time

I was angel-messenger, heisted up between
green marble floor and cobalt sky, revelling
in Godness and the surgent
confidence of the organ.
*

When I climbed down
from the upper reaches of myself,
when the slow Amen had trailed
its silken skirts away across the sanctuary,

I crept in behind the organ
to revel once again in dust and rust and dowels,
in cobwebs on the unadorned
vertebrae of the pipes; brought back to worm-holed boards

radiant in reflected colours off the rose window
with tales of the one Source, the walking-on-red-dust roads
of the Christ, of the Love-dancer
whom the whole globe of earth could not enclose.

NIGHT PRAYER

Rembrandt: Landscape with the Rest on the Flight into Egypt

I

This, too, you see, is prayer, these words I labour to admit
    under the spirit's prompting, words on the notebook
    difficult to decipher, the ink flowing out too fast

in the first stirrings; pen, copybook and keyboard
    in an attempt to touch the source of light,
    of life, the groundwork of our hope. Here, too,

II

figures in a nightscape, a pause in the difficult journey;
           questions
    of resting in penumbra, of knowing light is fragile,
    like a child holding its greedy mouth to the breast;

there is a fire of sticks, trouvaille of twig and branch, to keep
    wolves at bay, (between here and destination, Emmaus, say,
    beyond a life's full circle, light against the darkness) and this

III

is Jesus, name and nature of our source and sustenance, this
    is God, dwarfed by trees and distances, enormous landscape
    and a darkening night, and you grow aware that here the

watchful small lamps of greed and power are looming over all.
   The canvas, too, is prayer, impasto, brush and palette knife,
   working to ease the blackness about the light, cognisant

IV

of the death of innocents; it is all self-portrait, still life, a halt
   in the hastening, the helplessness of humankind before
           its own,
   the helplessness of God trusting Himself to flesh;

love is a small child, far from consciousness, hunted;
           should he be
   found and killed, what then? what then? Rembrandt
   knew that distance between himself and God
           – all time, all space, all

V

life, all death – had been too great; the instruments of art,
           sharpened and
   softened in the desiring heart, shorten the distance, finding
   a sheltering tree, light shouldering the darkness; this

Egypt of the imagination, this den of safety called
   exile, as world with its instruments of power and economics
   preys on you and how can you believe your pigments

VI

touch beyond impossibility? Image, less real than
 thistledown in a western gale, less permanent
   than golden light
 reflected on a pond, you try to empty the ocean of silence

with the holding power of pigments, the silence that is God.
 Christ-beyond-all-grasping, the heart in its pleading
   is a series
 of shifting darkscapes, vaulted in night-prayer passageways.

THE PRIDE OF LIFE

for Tim Sheehan

McGarvey and I were young and male and speaking
of the concupiscence of eyes, of flesh,
of the pride of life; our God, old Taskmaster,
demanded of us perfection, suffering and Latin.

McGarvey and I were dressing boards
of flesh-coloured deal, dovetailing them
into library shelves when the chisel,
curved like the quarter moon, slipped, and sliced

into my index finger; maladroit, I watched
blood spurt until the pain scalded me
and I sat down, stunned, amongst wood-shavings
and white dust; *in illo tempore* seminarians,

McGarvey and I (like Christ himself) were in otherwhere
on carpentry assignment, though I was more
for the study of Aquinas and the Four Last Things, more
apt with pen and paper and the ancient texts;

my finger-flesh had lifted and I tied it, tight,
with my seminarian's white handkerchief – *you're
pale as a ghost*, McGarvey said, that ghost
still with me now, pen in hand, wandering the world,

a fine-curved scar on my index finger;
a solitary gladiolus, elegant and tall,
of a cardinal brightness, beckons to me
from outside the window, and that young seminarian –

misfit and eager, trenchant and melancholy
in the pursuit of love – haunts me still, his God
and McGarvey's God, displaced, replaced, my God
untonsured now, and feminine, and here.

A BIRTH

Yeshua, at your birth, did the angels
sing Vivaldi's *Gloria*? and the shepherds,
did they play jaws harp, Jews' harp, tonguing
Dvořák's *New World Symphony*? The spheres —
were they humming, as twilight turned from
tangerine to emerald, and down
to a drear and turquoise basso — did the stars
sound out Bruckner, Brahms and Bach?
That sheep may safely graze ... Or was it merely
the snuffling of animals in their stalls, dawn-music
played each morning in the small farms, the opening
of stable doors, or city-sounds of preparation
for another day, like an orchestra tuning up, this
puer natus, this image of love, of God invisible.

NAME AND NATURE

Your name, Jesus, is childhood in the body, at times
a single malt upon the tongue, Vivaldi to the ears;

your name, Christ, forgiveness to the heart, acceptance
to the flesh, a troubled joy across the soul;

at ever my very best I will plead to you, closest to me,
for kindness. Perhaps the silence I take for God's

non-presence is the noise in which I have immersed
my life; nor have I framed a quiet to correspond

to His, where I might find my every call
answered. I seek kind. You are the reality I cling to,

the flesh, the history, the spurting out of blood. I believe
the non-attendance of my God lies in my absence from Him

and He is present, like the embrace of air
or the inward forces of the seasons. Your name, Jesus,

is the river on which I float, your name, Christ, the ocean
where everything is in place, is shivering, beautiful, and apart.

ENCOUNTER

It is March; in Ireland
daffodils will be suffering the harshest winds; here
the coach had turned back from the slopes of the Beatitudes
towards Tiberias; to the right

the valleys, green and flush,
rising to the hills; to the left, the lake, quietened
in an evening lull and pleasuring.
I settled in my seat, comforted, and tired; when —

and this is my wakeful dream, the happening, the real —
in the coach-seats opposite, father,
fisherman and March-month birthday-boy,
and brother, Declan,

impatient God-lover, picketer by the gates
of San Quentin, celebrant of falling free at last
from alcohol addiction: both of them
in animated conversation, both of them dead

for years, and months; they spoke
in a language without words, song-like, seductive.
Outside, darkness was falling early, the sun
a dying fire, light catching

on the thorn of the moon that was lying idle
in a sapphire-shaded heaven; soon there would be
        shimmering
silver nightways out across the sea. Father
suddenly called to me, and pointed; the bus

stopped, and we stepped down, we three, only;
silently they walked across the grass, down
towards the shore;
drawn, confused, I followed,

the light so faint now all was shadow,
father, old friend, and faithful; Declan, brother, and priest.
The old man turned to me, and smiled, "we", he said, "we
are not in death, we are in life".

He pointed. There was another
standing near the lake, her back to us, she was watching
out over the water, frail-boned, slight
but firm. "Mother?" I said and she turned,

slowly; I did not know her; fair-skinned,
handsome but not beautiful. "Your name?" I asked;
"Miryam", she said, "Miryam of Magdil. And yours?"
"Yohanan", I answered, to my surprise. Around us

ruins only, excavations, stone-heaps, stumps – Magdil?
"It was here," she said, "he
stepped ashore from the fishing-boat;
and stood awhile, gazing towards the hills; I

was kneeling, there, by that great rock;
I was gutting fish, for salting; I worried for his feet,
naked against the sharp edges of the shells;
the others, fishermen, moved awkwardly,

hauling the boat ashore, uncertain of themselves;
and "who are you?" I asked him
though I already knew the answer; he
is the way, he is the life, and his truth

will sear both soul and body. And he said, "Miryam",
as if he knew me; "if I give", he said,
"word of myself, what can that be to you? Come,
and see". And I left fish, and shore, lake and village

and followed him. He is invasion, hero, mystery,
he is the centre, he is forgiveness, light. "And now I," she said,
"am in death no longer, I am in life." She smiled,
turning back towards the sea;

I glanced for father, brother, but they were
not there and when I turned again, she, too, had disappeared.
I shivered suddenly, alone, and cold; a black-backed gull,
perched on the great rock,

was stabbing down
at some small feathered thing.
Now it was night;
from the road Abram was calling out to me

and I came back, at peace, heavy in flesh, but free.

WALLS

I stand – a continent away
from the crumbled walls of Bunnacurry 2-room school –
now, at last, by the Western Wall,
leaning my hands against its massive stones, and seeking words;

"in Yerushalayim", the Spirit wrote, "shall be my name forever";

to my left, black coat and pants,
white shirt and thick grey beard, kippah, prayer shawl, a man
sways back and forth in prayer –
hear, O Yisrael, The Lord our God, the Lord is one …
      Torah, psalms;

our little catechism asked: *does God*

know all things? The high partition
between the rooms squealed on its castors, folding open,
when Father Tiernan came
to test our souls; *God knows all things, even*

our most secret thoughts and actions. I relished then

the loveliness of the near-rhymes,
the old-fashioned *doth*-and-*dost* of the English, leaving
a softly-furred coating on the soul. I need to know
the rough texture of a wall you could break your life against;
      and so

I have come to take possession, of the songs, the psalms,
      the lamentations,

Ruth and Boaz, Jonah,
Daniel in the den of lions – for these are my stories, too,
the prophet Moshe stretching out his hand
over the sea, Yermiyahu's grief before the golden throne

of Babylon, with Markos, Mattityahu, Loukas, Yohanan ...

for here is the gate of Heaven, folded open,
where we thrust our words towards the invisible,
            waiting for those
inaudible answers, where we thrust our prayers
into the crevices in the wall,

and speak aloud, look, here I am, oh Elohim, oh Yeshua,
            here I am.

GOLDCREST

Of course they come back, the dead, because they are there,
just beyond our being, on the other side
of that nothingness we are scared of, because there is work
        to do,
on earth and in the heavens,

and because we haunt them. We hear the intricate
tock-tick-tock of the wound-tight
innards of creation: Laudate Dominum, Hagia Sophia,
        epistolary
symphonies of St Paul.

But our New God is not the Most High God :
he is Burning-bush and Whinny-hill and Furze-bloom; he is not
a gilt tabernacle bathed
in ethereal light – but goldcrest, flitting in the berberis

for a feast of insect while snow
flurries down through a wash of sunlight this out-of-season
Easter week. God
is not *not*, unchanging, unbegotten, ineffable, God is *is*. So I

– remembering days when the pink rose rambled,
and blackberries plashed purple kisses on my lips – find
contentment this side of nothingness, and being
ghosted by the presence of those I have loved, and lost.

TOWNLAND

Bethlehem: the village, and the townland,
crowded and expectant
like a fair day in Bunnacurry; in our dark cowhouse
there were snuffling sounds

and the warm, rich reek of cattle.
Bethlehem: Joseph and Mary standing,
wide eyes fixed on one another,
the whimper of a boy-child in between; brown earth outside

was frumped and sodden
under the slow breathing of mist. A harsh half-moon
shivered on the frosted road
down to the Bunnacurry church, and we, children,

bundled ourselves tight
in winter coats, our breathing forming angel-shapes
on the biting air. It was just a birth; one
out of millions that had come before, of millions

that would come after; this one birth
neither a beginning, nor an ending; a turning-point
merely, though shading all that went before, all
after, tossing the rags and peelings of time into the uncertain

texture of eternity. Bethlehem: stars
above the caverned escarpment. Crib and candle-light
in Bunnacurry chapel, where we knelt
awed by festival, by the silence surrounding, by the animals.

ACCORDING TO LYDIA

Cock-Crow

It was soon after dawn and he was out already,
raw and impatient, for we could hear his axe
splitting wood, the first dull dunts, then the quick
rupturing sound, its echo against the roosters' calls;
there was strength and such assurance in the sound
the village came to itself with a morning confidence;
the thousand-year-old olive stumps resisted stanchly,
but he would later polish the wood to a perfection
smooth to the thumb. By noon he'd pause, listening
to the laughter of young girls busying themselves
among the vines. Then, in the afternoon loafing-hours,
he would slip away to some hidden wilderness
alone, as if fruits of earth and toil were slight. A shadow
would darken the woman's face watching from the doorway :

Bedrock

Wilderness. We heard first about locusts and wild
honey; then, demons and beasts. Sheer absences, no
water. Shade. Comfort. The sun so fiery that the low hills
shimmer like a mirage. There are cool, sheltering places,
occupied. Easy to believe in demons, so little sound
there the mind hums. By day the burning, by night
the crackle of frost; thudding stillness of the heart, admitting
wisdom, dust-awareness; immured in desert nothingness
and the struggle with the mind. Opening to loneliness,
to the holiness of the unresponding; garnering strength

against the worst that noon can do, or the trailing moon;
dying to flesh-hungers, earning a certainty
that washed him through with tenderness, that raked
spirit and flesh to a sheer, uncompromising love :

The Binding

The lake's edge – generation after generation
depending, shallow at the shores, bronzewater, gold;
millennia of shells, patterned dull and gay, becoming grit –
profound, a harvest, what's left of innumerable deaths.
They have drawn the boats up onto the grass, and sit
examining the nets; the human heart, they know, is forged
out of such bindings, such husks, at the very lip
of wilderness. This day, out of a sky so bright
it chafes like silver, they hear the high-pitched cry
of a swooping sea-eagle ripping the air. The man –
in mulberry-coloured robe and leathern sandals – has passed
down along the margins towards the boats; at once
there is disturbance, a sharp kerfuffle at the lake's edge
and the brothers, without a backward glance, forsake the shore :

Kfar Nahum

Beyond the village, willows, scrub grass, small waves
frivolously fingering the shore; warm breeze under grey,
scarce shifting, clouds; the day lifeless, and everyday
ordinary; a fishing-boat drawn up onto stones,
no shore-birds visible; noon, as if the world had
paused, uncertain, waiting. In the crumbling synagogue

craftsmen and fishermen sat, bemused, the stranger
standing before them, reading, and expounding; as if he bore
quietness in his bones in spite of the earthed resonance
in his voice; the authority, the unaccountable wisdom
that had been concealed somewhere in the Torah scrolls,
the mourners, the merciful, the hungry. Puzzlement
among them, here and there a muttering anger. Words,
as ours, but new, and other. A man like us. Unlike. But like :

Disturbances

By sunset, in Kfar Nahum, he had drawn to himself
many of the broken, crazed and trodden-down,
the undesirables, the pariahs and the freaks;
the space between gate and lake was a market-field
of clamour, pleading, incredulity and tears. Soon
he was exhausted. A yellow moon
hoisted itself slowly above the village, and a crow,
lifting in dudgeon out of the roost, called a loud
craw! to the clouds. By now, we were unsure of it,
what had happened, for something difficult
was insinuating itself within the stepped-out limits
of our life, but we knew there would be consequences,
grave. It was owl-night, the bird calling out "who? who?";
can what is broken be whole again, what's crooked straight :

The Flowering

That night we lit lamps everywhere, outside, within,
on grass and pathway, down to the shore; he sat on,

all light and shadow, his words gathering radiance
and darkness into their texture; we lived a while in an island
of being, apart, and unmanageable; and oh! the strangeness:
a cock crowing, bright-winged moths singeing themselves
against the flames; smoke from the oils sometimes
itched the eyes but we stayed, startled when he said: *your
sins are forgiven!* and no-one, there and then, doubted it –
we thought of our blessed YHWH; we thought of the stone
heads and torsos of gods in the city set on their shaky
pedestals, and the night swelled; as if the raw green stem
of the Pentateuch were about, latterly, to open into
a great red wound, like the high and blossoming amaryllis :

Demons

It takes a lifetime to cast demons out;
you struggle with them, you, demoniac, you, unclean,
they throw you down, you howl inside, you get
up again, you have to. Lest they destroy you. He
touched them, lepers, too, their sores, their bandages,
their dead eyes. He would take all burdens on himself.
Thirsted and hungered have we, for such as he, to enter
into the soul's holding. I have found, down in my heart,
there is a sphere so still, so silent and untouched
it is pure as the snow-topped summit of Hermon
glistening in the distance. He came, gathering them all to table,
the manic, the castaways, the hobbled (we thought him mad)
and there was laughter, and quiet and – I tell you this –
peace where never there was peace, nor laughter ever :

Table

I need to tell of this, I need to set it down –
how he brought them in with him, and how they grinned
at the shaken host; servants, with disdain, offered water
for their hands and feet but the stranger knelt and
helped them: the beggars, the bedraggled, and the whores;
they reclined on cushions at the rich man's table: who did not
eject them, offering lamb and artichokes and goat's cheese,
wine and pickled fish and pastries soused in honey; they
asked for barley bread and barley beer. The stranger broke
and dipped the bread and passed it to them, told them jokes
and stories of lost sheep and prodigals and wheat seeds
        scattered
against the wind. It was, the host adjured, a ghostly meal,
        touched him
with joy and bitterness, this kingdom rife with casualties –
but it was I, he said, who found I was immured in poverty :

Samaria

Jacob's well, Shechem, route of nomads, revolt, crusade …
of people toiling down valleys of silence into exile: she
drawing near – heart torn by love-failures – to the source now,
the sustenance. The stranger, waiting; out of exodus and genesis
with demanding words. Between them, issues of time,
        of history,
the depths of the iced-over, petrified heart. "I thirst":
        who, then,
is keeper of the soul in need: he, or she?
        Between them, between

past and future, the clarity of water in the moment of its
giving, words echoing beyond the sound of words,
      beyond clanging
of consonant, bird-call of vowel, how the heart,
      in its taut holding,
wants to yield, to the presence, the immediacy. She, later,
returning home, stumbles, her pitchers full. He
stays, on the ridge of stone, staring down into the deep
till the moon brightens, down there, in the uttermost
      darkness :

Papyrus

The word, I have discovered, is food for my surviving,
this need to lay down words on strong papyrus, in strait
and patterned lines, hints of love and yearning, and now
this penchant towards sorrowing, for memory is uncertain, inaccurate, and, like waters, fluid. Words of Yeshua
who sought to slip away, before dawn, to a desert place,
      to touch
his source and sustenance. For after all, after that mid hour,
my life will not be what it was; what, then, had happened?
      The word
existence seemed to shift, as boulders shift in a quake,
      the straight
line of living twisted back upon itself in a kind of anguish,
what we had accomplished suddenly became undone, the
comfortable dark was now backlit by a more aggressive fire –
for he had stood, tears on his cheeks, before the sealed tomb;
he called: and there was a death-silence: I heard a hum
of insects, somewhere the sharp howl of a jackal, an echo

out of Lethe and in the heat of noon my body chilled;
slowly, they unsealed the tomb, stood at its gaping mouth
mute in darkness; the sisters clutched each other, terrified.
He emerged, slow, slow, shrouded in white cotton, like a great
woodcock with folded wings, body camouflaged in snow,
and it was I who called, out of a living hope within me,
fly high! Lazarus, fly! But he stood still: perplexed, perhaps
blinded by the sun, when the sisters moved to him,
   and the crowd
astounded, cried with a shrill ululation, like flocks of startled
shore-birds until he stood, freed, and moved towards Yeshua
like a lover stepping out in exaltation. I understood there is
   no such thing
as the ordinary world, that words themselves are not
transparent, and I became, just then, afraid of this man
   of men :

Mediterranean

Came that day on the beach; Yeshua stood a long while
and spoke, of love, of mercy, of tenderness; and my spirit
sang again. We grew hungry. There he was,
   frying fish over stones,
with garlic, oil, fresh bread, and I could not figure
from where came all that food. There were sea winds, and each
morsel that we ate spoke benevolence while the ocean,
   behind us,
murmured its assent. He had his place now in my heart, no,
   it was
even deeper than the heart. We had come for pleasure,
   what we took

was the scent of the sea, a sense of comfort mixed with dread,
the sunset pink of flamingos flying over.

I remember the new port,
breakwaters, the Roman galleys, new economies; the stranger –
Yeshua – had taken spittle on his fingers and touched the eyes
of a blind man; but Yeshua had mentioned fear and we saw,
beyond the grasses and wild flowers a small group,

hostile, gathering :

The Garden

Dusk – the sun going down – threw long shadows across
the ground. He appeared, coming from the valley, and collapsed
on the hard earth; somewhere a bird sang, though the word
"chuckled" came to mind. I remembered Genesis: the Lord God
walking in the garden, time of the evening breezes. An hour
passed; the world darkened further; up in the city
lights flickered. I thought I heard sobbing, even a scarcely
suppressed cry. He rose, and moved, stumblingly, back
towards the wall; I heard voices, protestations. Then he came
to fall again, scrambling on earth as if his bones were fire
and though I sensed rather than saw his body, he was distorted
like limbs of the olive trees. I heard weeping; I heard fingers
scrabbling against ground. Weakness, and failure; embarrassing.
Relief to see the flare of torches coming this way from

the city :

The Viewing

When he was harried out to be jeered at, blood-
ugly, rag-scraggly, filthy with sores, I knew
he must be guilty and I was ashamed. He could
scarcely hold himself erect, they jostled him,
there was blood congealing on his face, his
fingers, even on his naked, blistering feet. He had no
hope, he was already stooped amongst the dead.
Like a fool he stayed silent, stubbornly so, though
words could not save him now. This was degradation
before the people, who mocked his agonies, his death,
the ultimate humiliation, for even rats
will creep away to die, in private, in a dark
corner. We knew now that his name would be
forgotten, left with his corpse in merciful oblivion :

Hill of Skulls

(i)
I stood on the slope, at a distance from the other women;
it was done on the Hill of Skulls, dread place, to discourage
thought; high posts planted, waiting for the cross-
branches, the flower, and the fruit, where the dead earth
was rusted over with spilled blood; a little aside –
though within eye-shot – from the city's bustle
            and indifference.
Miryam, for it must be she, stood propped between strength
and failure, determined mother to the last. I had dreamed
he would put an end to violence. The big iron nails
were not the worst, though the heavy hammer-blows

shuddered the earth and shuddered my heart – it was the body
writhing in agony, chest strained beyond the possible at each
in-breath, out-breath, it was how humankind spits hatred
against its own, the tender-hearted, innocent, the children –
　　　　but

(ii)
it's how things are, the soldier said, and will always be.
The moments passed, each one dragging as an hour; I tried
prayer, but to whom, or to what? The sky darkening,
　　　　the groans
lengthening, the screams. . . He was burning.
　　　　　　Near us the cackling
magpies. In the sky, the vultures. The way, he had said,
the truth, the life – is the way death, then? Life, the urgencies
only of the body? And truth, what is truth? His blood
mingling on the earth with blood of the contemned. Love
the final casualty. Clouds blackened; hot winds
blew in across the hill, shadows were dancing wildly
amongst confused noises. He cried out, though rarely. My
tears were silent, copious. I heard a distant, drawn-out
thunder. After such hours he screamed out, died; as if
he had exhaled, with his last breath, all the light and

(iii)
life of the world. Thunderstorms as they took
him down, as I hurried through the streets people
were staggering by, like ghosts. I never felt so
much alone. That was the most muted evening,
night was black and long and I armed myself about
with fires of spitting olive-wood; in the laneways skulked
furtive shapes; I clung, desperately, to the supposed

mercy of time; words had lost essence and would spill
like hot grease. How could the world know he had lived, how
could the word love be redefined? Everything unfinished, all
undone. But I had inks, formed out of soot and oil and tears
and would carve deep in the papyrus. I remember – back then
on the mountainside – he had said: those of singleness of heart
will be blessed, for it is they who will see God :

Sunrise

So clear we had not grasped it: in the giving away of life
you find it. Soon after dawn I was leaning on the stone walls
of the vineyard out beyond the city. There was a well, timbers
covering it; I heard the wood rattling; there was a man
stooping over, reaching for a drink; he saw me, called out
something, waved, and was gone. Tricks of the light, I thought,
the sudden wing-claps of doves distracting. I stayed, fingers
worrying the clay between the stones. I had not even
waved back. Bright this early and I imagined the valley
singing softly. The intimacy of grape-flesh, I thought, the skin
peeled off, the dark wine waiting. The mind can find itself
so foolish, hoping for too much. The quickening of a heart
urgent against grief. Or urgent towards unutterable
joy. And I stood there, stood, baffled again by this one life :

The Turning

After the killing, there was no hope left, nowhere
to turn. We abandoned the city, wondering if we might
get somewhere. Sat, disconsolate, by the river, knowing

how goodness appears and is vanquished before it is
clasped. Wondering if there is a way for mortal beings
to start over. Someone, walking the same path, may offer
wisdom, and insight. Becomes, in the nonce, mediator
between place and non-place, life not-life, death and
not-death. The day advancing, our steps more sprightly,
we would hold to light against the nightfall. That someone ...
Logs blown to flames in the hearth; dried fish, olives, figs
and honeyed wine; the ready warmth of love, the torn hands
blessing and breaking bread. What the blood had known
known now in spirit and for truth. And so we turned :

Lydia

I fear onslaughts of foolishness before the end,
the loss of wonder when the mind cools, the wine
ordinary, the bread bread. Do not fear, he said, only
believe. I work to keep the heart open, glory in the once-fire
that will be ash, in reason beyond reason. I work to cherish
the variegated birdsong, the damson flowers blossoming
when they will. That I may ever overflow with Yeshua,
as a jug will overbrim with a wine both sweet and bitter.
I know I will meet him again, the raw wounds of humanity
on his flesh. I remember the sea's edge, when, late evening,
he spoke from the fishing-boat anchored just off-shore: See
and hear as a child, he said, that the deaf hear and the blind
have their eyes opened, the lame walk and the dead rise again
and blessed is the one who does not lose faith in me.

AIDAN: A LIFE

Connacht born, lean and intent, he prayed –
may all that you are, Jesus, live in me;

child-spine already strengthening upwards, he reached
for the strict and straitened life of islands –

the Arans, Iona, Lindisfarne. He would be
adept in new languages, out of Gaelic into English,

out of flesh and into Jesus. He grew itinerant,
travelling through the smalltowns, fishing villages,

a black flame visible along the causeway, embracing
the Christ-fire to his chest. Autumn, and festival,

foison in the fields and villages, apples, hazels, farm-scents,
calls of the Brent geese from the marshes, flotillas

of Eider riding the inshore waves; and Aidan's harvesting
rising slowly to heaven like a white smoke, because the last

of this earth's people, caps in hand, expect for themselves no
miracles, only their daily bread, a modicum of peace.

NAMING OF THE BONES

London, June 2017

I looked up and saw you, your distorted body
writhing again in agony. There is a season, the Big Book says,

a time to die, a time to weep, and a time for peace;
no one, it says, can understand what is happening
                under the sun.

I saw the bare breast heaving, that once beautiful breast;
I hurt for you, for your beloved once beautiful, body,
                each twist or twitch,

each reach and wrench adds to the fire in your flesh
and bones. I plead to creator lover God for you,
                to ease your pain,

to mother you. I wince once more at the bitter-spittle angers
of humankind: the blunted iron nails driven through
                your caring hands,

your tender feet; so that impossible you hang from them, and
stand on them; the muscles cramp and spasm, and your face,

so beautiful once, is contorted with spit and ugliness, with
blood and sweat and tears. Today, my Christ, June 14,
                twenty-seventeen,

Grenfell Tower in London was engulfed in flames; inestimable
furnace, suffering unbearable. A child appears for a moment,
                at a window

of the sixteenth floor, a moment only, frantic, waving:
to a not-there-saviour; you? We hurt, my Christ, we hurt.
                    Why is our spittle

hot with bitterness? Words, the Big Book says, can be
wearisome, a chasing after wind. And yet ... the world breaks.
                    The world

re-forms. But the beautiful body breaks, and yields.
Yearning and grief trouble us. At the heart of it.
                    You. Hurting.

TRADING PLACES

rain down, you heavens, from above

The way up into the hayloft was a wooden ladder
cruel with splinters; it rose
rough-hewn and steep, out of the stable, cows snuffling

in bulked contentment, and lowing softly; above
in a fragrant gloom, hay dust tickled me
into satisfying sneezes. I lay back, alert and absent,

lazing between earth and heaven, watched the wraiths
and angels in the rafters,
imaginary mouths unspeaking, bats above them, twitching

their black-silk presences. Morning, I was slop-sloshing
water, yard-brushing dung out under the rains.
Near midnight I heard – ringing from the choir-loft
       – *rorate coeli*

desuper et nubes fluant justum. I knelt before the manger, sensing
that everything – moon, kneeler, a mistle-thrush's
tracks on the snow – was now more than ever it had been,
          peace

possible amongst us, tenderness, and love. The Word
had wakened into the being of our world,
the unspeakable become verb, translatable. Language become

humanity's return to divinity, the infant's high-register cries,
the syrinx of a singing bird, all
framing one sentence, a staircase rising towards the heavens.

THE GATE

Sometimes, towards dusk, when the winds
come buffeting from the east, the Holy Ghost slips in
through the red bars with a loud sigh,
brings a cold shivering near the heart and leaves me
restless. These nights – as the world faces its nightmares

under the weight of coronavirus – I think I hear
the reassuring and unsettling surges of the sea –
not the rough, unpredictable waters of Atlantic Ocean
but waves of grasses under the breeze
and gracious meadows wild with buttercups.

When, late evening, I lean on the topmost bar
of the red gate, looking out on the shadowed world,
I search the innermost reaches of the spirit, scared
lest I discover emptiness, a well that has run dry and holds
only woodlice and weevils in its depths;

but then I have swung round with joy
to hear the scratchy song of the whitethroat
as it rises from a fence and flies
low and fast into a field; I know a gratitude
that tells of the sacred otherness of the earth.

There is a rusty and twisted nail
hammered in the top hinge of the gate
to stop it scraping across the tarmac drive;
a tiny golden earwig hides in the battered bolt-hole;
but the red gate is frontier and boundary, embrace

of the within and the without, eye of the needle,
its blood-red criss-crossing the entrance
into, and out of, life. Inside the gate I release the words
like variegated moths held fluttering in my hands
and hope they will not fly in vain; I have engaged

with the enticing poetry of the Christ,
and been engrossed in the cosmic wisdom
of this anointed world, its weathers and renewals,
involved in the exasperated, creating spirit
of humankind. Sometimes, after dusk,

the words failing, with darkness swelling
from the woods, I think my spirit may slip out
through the red gate of the sheepfold, will find
the narrow road – and with a profound sigh
soar away towards a long-anticipated rest.

OMEGA

(Offrande, et alléluia final)

Late-winter evening, I heard the monks intone
the *Salve Regina*, pleading with the advocate
before nightfall; like distant seashore sounds
the voix celeste on the organ ... *nunc dimittis*,
a God-haunted, nebulous and compelling chant
fills all the dimlit naves of the world. Tonight,
with moonlight polishing the waves to steel,
I iterate my offering: words from the heart,
to dedicate the music, and the life, to the one
Word, to the wholeness of being. The pages
become scrawled with words, at times so fast I can't
read them; sometimes they are like spring
water, down by James's Rock, so much overgrown
the mouth of the well has disappeared. Better
to void this slackening mind, to wait upon the Spirit
counsellor. I watched, against a darkening
tangerine sky, a wedge of swans, eleven, twelve,
flying low over the valley, their wings sounding
like the breathing of an old pump-organ,
and all the earth was sentient: nazard, gamba,
dulciana – and I imagined all the birds of the world,
their feathers coloured apricot, indigo
and blue as they intone creation's own Gregorian,
all the birds, like bells, like alleluia, like the evening
flute-song of the blackbird. I inhaled the wonder,
bent my body towards the ground, whispering –
alleluia, amen amen oh Christ, our Christ, amen.

JAMES HARPUR

THE FLIGHT OF THE SPARROW

"My lord, although we cannot know
The mysteries of the afterlife
The span of time we spend on earth
Appears to me to be like this:
Imagine sitting in your hall
In winter, feasting with your chiefs
And counsellors – your faces glowing
From flames that crackle in the hearth.
Outside, the wintry night is lashed
By winds and driving rain and snow.
Suddenly a sparrow darts in
Through a door, flits across the hall
And flies out through another one.
Inside, cocooned in light and warmth
It can enjoy a moment's calm
Before it vanishes, rejoining
The freezing night from which it came.
Such is our journey through this life.
But as to what's in store for us
Beyond the doors of birth and death
We are completely in the dark."

from Bede, *The History of the English People*, 2.13

A VISION OF COMETS

The flight was delayed.
Outside, the night sky was clear
And the land that had received the sun all day
Now slept in silence.
It could have been a Greek island
Or the new land of America.
He was returning home, for good, or for bad,
And the welter of accumulated memories
And friendships loomed up from the pit
Of his stomach in sudden queasy waves.
Time ticked on and passengers sat in rows
Under the flickerings of neon
Slowly numbing themselves to the worry
Of wondering when the flight would flash up.
Eventually, sunk in the midst of
Painful feelings of regret and loss
A sense of peace overtook him
An inner inexplicable assurance
That his journey home was right.
He felt suddenly at ease and, turning round,
Saw people rising as one from their seats
Quickly assembling their luggage and moving
Towards the gate for their departure.
He went back against the flow to find his bags
And say goodbye to those who had been his intimates.
But as he made his way to where he'd been
He saw what seemed to be starry darkness –
As if the wall had melted away –
And people vanishing into the fringes of his eyes.

He somehow knew the young man who stood there.
It must have been outside for the darkness
Stretched around, sealing the horizons.
He approached the man, who pointed to the sky
And there, igniting the dark in golden sprays,
Eight glowing comets moved softly through the night
Slowly rising, turning, dipping, gliding
Like gilded dolphins hooping through a sea of blue.
Their tails, from which auras of sparkle
Would fizz and fade, were interwoven and moving
As if guided by an intelligence
As if the comets were on the kite strings controlled
By this young man as he moved his hands.
Then the comets began dissolving –
Yet their particles realigned and coalesced
Into luminous strokes with dots and squiggles –
And he realised they were giant words of Hebrew,
That they were telling him what his purpose was,
What his mission was on earth.

THE FALCON CAROL

The falcon flew from dark to dark
Drew silver from the Northern Star
And headed for the crinkled hills,
The rivers, lakes and waterfalls
    To find the source of light on earth
    The source of light on earth.

And as three weary pilgrim kings
Looked up and saw his glittering wings
The falcon saw a darkened town
A stable glowing like a crown
    And knew that he had found the truth
    That he had found the truth.

The falcon hovered like a star
His wings spun out a spirit fire
That drew the kings inside the shed:
The child asleep in his straw bed
    Was dreaming of a silver bird
    Was dreaming of a bird.

His task now done, the falcon rose
A spark ablaze with joyful news;
He lit the stars, he lit the moon
Then vanished in the arc of sun
    That dawned beyond the Southern Cross
    Beyond the Southern Cross.

"I STRETCH MY ARMS"

I stretch my arms like a swan flying
And watch, weightless, the world turning
So high up I can see – it seems without end
The city of Rome, the snowy alps
Triremes of Alexandrian traders
Pearl-divers practising from rocks
The wind wandering through the wilderness.
I am rooted to the spot, rotting inside
The sun casts no shadow of the compass
I had no choice but to choose this perch
And now I cannot choose any more
Each choice I made was like a nail
Fixing my arms to embrace the world.

from JOSEPH OF ARIMATHEA

One night I saw him in a dream
As clear and potent as a vision
Walking upon the tops of waves,
All white and crinkling in the moon,
And leading tiny silver fish
In shifting shoals beneath his feet
And multiplying all the time –
I saw their myriad scales of light
Beneath the surface of the sea
Shimmering in swathes of light
Like fields of grain swept by wind
And felt their radiance – I knew
They were the essence of creation
The particles of life itself
Gathering and then separating
And swirling into other patterns
That glittered with intelligence
Like flocks of birds or swarms of bees
Or thoughts appearing in a mind
Before rejoining into one –
I felt my being was that sea
An ocean teeming, tingling
With every form of living thing
Or rather I should say there was
A feeling of divinity
Because there was no "I" to feel
But simply simple radiance
Complete, absorbing and unending …
And then he spoke to me and said:

"The body dies but love lives on
In measure with your life on earth.
Everyone is responsible
And every act of kindness made
While you are still alive
No matter how half-heartedly
Or small and insignificant
Strengthens the universal ties
That flow between each living thing –
The stones and trees and animals
And every single human being –
And link this world with all the stars:
Love makes the cords of light
Increase in luminosity
Until the ceiling of the night
Becomes a dome of radiance
And this is heaven, this is heaven …
The great ingathering of life
Fulfilled at last through holy love
In which there is no separation
For what you see is what you are
And what you are is what you see –
For all is God, and God is one."

CRANBORNE WOODS
(17 MAY, 1994)

For my mother

We stopped the car, ducked below the fence
Felt time unravelling in a revelation
The seconds fall and scatter into thousands

Of tiny saints, a reborn multitude
Flowing past the trees, through pools of sun,
Each earthly form a spirit flame, pure blue.

They watched us drift among them, large as gods,
As if we'd come as part of their parousia
To stay with them forever in these woods.

As time grew darker we slipped away like ghosts
And slowly drove ... towards your death next May
When once again I saw the risen host

Could watch you walking weightlessly among
The welcomers, the gently swaying throng.

CORN CIRCLE

For my father

It was the third day after he was dead
His body yet to be consigned to fire
We were marooned in limbo, as becalmed

As the endless days of summer rolling by,
Turning to ash the surface soils of Wiltshire
And shrinking the chalk streams of our valley.

That evening we stood on Pepperbox Hill
Gazing at fields embalmed in golden heat
And there, as if cut from the corn, a circle.

We walked down and picked our way through rows
Towards the solar disc burning in the wheat
And crossed the threshold of the temenos

Entering the benediction of the stasis
The heart of the sun, whirling, motionless.

THE WHITE SILHOUETTE

For John F. Deane

"There went a whisper round the decks one morning, 'We have a mysterious passenger on board'. . . Often I thought of that rumour after we reached Jerusalem . . . When I saw the man all in white by the Golden Gate carrying in all weathers his lighted lamp, I always thought, 'There is a mysterious pilgrim in Jerusalem'."

> Stephen Graham, from *With The Russian Pilgrims to Jerusalem* (1913)

I thought we would meet in a holy place
Like the church in the hamlet of Bishopstone
Empty on a Wiltshire summer's day
The trees full of rooks and hung in green
And the stream in the meadows a rush
Of darkling silver beneath the bridge
Where I saw my first kingfisher flash
Its needle, leaving its turquoise stitch
In my memory. And I would sit
In the church and close my eyes
And wait in vain for something to ignite,
And wonder whether this was my life
Wasting away in my mother's home.
Sometimes I'd bring Herbert's *Temple*
And read the quiet order of his poems
And picture him, as once he was glimpsed,
Hugging the floor in his church at Bemerton
Asking love to bid him welcome.
I sat with an upright praying disposition
Preoccupied in self-combing

Too callow and spiritually impatient
To notice if you had slipped in
As a tourist to inspect the choir or font
And buy a picture postcard and sign
The book with "lovely atmosphere";
Or as a walker taking refuge from rain
Or a woman primping flowers by the altar.

Or somewhere like the island of Patmos
Out of season and the tourist flow,
The sea leeching blue from the skies.
In the cave of St John, pointillist gold
On tips of candles and highlights of icons,
You might have visited that day in September
When I was there, absorbing the coolness,
Imagining John on the Day of the Lord
Prostrate on the ground as if before a throne
And you not dressed in a "robe and gold sash"
Nor with hair "as white as wool or snow"
But as a pilgrim with camera and rucksack
Respectful, curious, guide-book in hand
Appreciating the grain of raw stone
Catching my eye and pausing for a second
As if I were a schoolfriend from years ago.
I never saw you, if you were there,
For I was too blinded by the new Jerusalem
Flashing out jasper, topaz, sapphire,
Descending from heaven like a huge regal crown.

Or somewhere like Holycross in Tipperary,
The abbey at the meeting of road and river,
You might have stopped to break a journey
As I often do, and seen me there in the nave
Ambling down the sloping floor
Towards the relic-splinter of the Cross
Or sitting outside on the banks of the Suir
On a bench on a swathe of tended grass
Perhaps that day when, heading north,
I paused by the car park to watch
A bride, fragile, and frozen by the door
Her bridesmaids huddled in the cold of March
Waiting and waiting to make her entrance
Into the sudden shine of turning faces
Like a swan gliding in its snowdress
From an arch of the bridge in a state of grace.
I was too mesmerised by her destiny
To see you start your car, drive off,
And raise your hand as you passed me by
On the way to Cashel, Fermoy and the south.

But there was that time I was so certain
That I had finally found you;
Sick at home, I turned to meditation
And prayer to overcome self-pity
For weeks accumulating quietude
Till that morning when seconds were emptied out
My thoughts cleansed, my self destroyed
Within an uncanny infusing light
That seemed to deepen and unfold
More layers of radiance and lay me wide open
So you could cross the threshold

Or I could cross, at any moment.
But I closed the door of my heart, afraid,
Who knows, that I might have met you,
Afraid I would pass to the other side
And never return to all that I knew;
I thought I could always re-open myself
And greet you properly, well prepared.
I never did. I feared that sudden shift
Into the zone of timelessness; too scared
I looked for you in public, for safety,
I kneeled in churches, gave the sign
Of peace in St James's Piccadilly;
I recited prayers, took bread and wine
And I concentrated so hard, but failed
To believe they were your blood and body;
I heard staccato prayers, like nails
Banged in, as if to board up windows.

Sometimes I'd sense you as a glimmer
As in that dream I once had out of the blue
When you stood at night on a Greek island shore;
Your face was hidden, but it was you;
The stars pinned in place the layers of darkness;
Then came the comets, perhaps a dozen,
Their tails fanned out with diminishing sparks;
Slowly they twisted and turned – your hands
Moving in concert, as if you were guiding them,
As if they were on strings, like Chinese kites.
The comets slowed and stopped, and changed
Into letters of Hebrew, emblazoning the night.
And I knew if I could grasp those words,
Your silent message across the stars,

I'd know my destiny on earth.
Instead I woke, as puzzled as Belshazzar.

I do not search for you any more
I don't know whom to seek, or where;
Too weary, disillusioned, I'm not sure
What I think or if I really care
That much; my last hope – that my resignation
Might be a sign of the Via Negativa,
A stage of my self-abnegation –
Prevents the thing it hopes for.

And yet

I still write to you, poem after poem,
Trying to shape the perfect pattern
Of words and the mystery of their rhythm,
An earthly music audible in heaven –
Each poem is a coloured flare
A distress signal, an outflowing
Of myself, a camouflaged prayer
dispatched towards the Cloud of Unknowing
And all I have to do is stay
Where I am, ready to be rescued
Not move, speak or think but wait
For the brightening of the Cloud
For your white silhouette to break
Free from it and come nearer, nearer,
Till I see your essence and I can ask
Where in the world you were
Throughout my days – and only then
Will I grasp why I never found you

Because you were too close to home
Because I thought I'd have to die
To see you there, right there, removing
The lineaments of your disguise –
My careworn wrinkled skin
My jaded incarnation of your eyes –
My face becoming your face
My eyes your eyes
I   you   us   I you us
Iesus.

from ST SYMEON STYLITES

Most days I think I'm split in two.
A spirit yearning for the light
And a body of delinquent appetites
I tame by standing stiff all day,
Watching its scraggy silhouette
Revolve around me slowly
Waiting for hesitation, weakness.
I set my will against my flesh
But when the sun is swallowed up
I join the dark, become a shade
Within the filthy anarchy of dreams;
Helpless, adrift, I'm turned nightlong
Around the memory column of my sins.

At dawn I wake, bursting to feel the joy
Of Noah floating free towards
A shining uncontaminated world.
But when the sun erupts
I am a tatty raven in a nest
Of sand, hair, albino faeces
And bread rinds a half-wit monk
Lobs up to me with water-skins –
A wingless creature dreaming of flight
Feeling the desert cram inside me
Every loneliness I've ever known.

The desert's fields of nothing
Are giant mirrors of my soul
Reflecting every scrap of sin;
The more I purge myself
The more the specks crawl out
Like ants I stamp to death in rage –
How can God love my shrinking flesh,
My frailty, lack of constancy?
Why does he wait to strike me down?
I bow a thousand times a day –
At night I stay awake to pray
And pray to stay awake.
Sometimes I wonder if I pray
To keep the Lord away?

COLUMBA'S VISION

At certain times   my soul   unpeels itself
And I see the darkness   thinning
And I feel a lightness   lightening
And I can see   the universe –
This world   the flash of grass
A sudden swaying   residues of green;
At night   the great furnace
Flinging sparks   across the dark –
Too vast for waking comprehension ...
Then all draws tight
Into
a
single
blade
of
light.

BRENDAN

The naked hermit, cliffs of ice, the cold,
The island of the saints emerging from
Black fog as light, its shore of powdered gold

And apples ripening in every orchard
The youth who welcomed each of us by name –
These died around the settled fires of Clonfert.

But Judas on his rock, wind-burnt, stripped wise,
Writhing above the slaughter of the sea
Remains pristine inside my deepest darkness

His eyes alert for the approach of demons –
I see them glowing as when we rowed away
And hear his voice above the raucous ocean,

"Hell is stasis, keep heading for the sun
And when you reach the light, sail on, sail on."

KEVIN AND THE BLACKBIRD

I never looked, but felt the spiky feet
Prickling my outstretched hand. I braced my bones,
My heart glowed from the settling feathered heat

And later from the laying of the eggs
Heavy, as smooth and round as river-rolled stones,
Warm as the sun that eased my back and legs.

When I heard the cheepings, felt the rising nest
Of wings, the sudden space, the cool air flow
Across my fingers, I did not know the test

Had just begun – I could not bend my arms
But stood there stiff, as helpless as a scarecrow,
Another prayer hatching in my palms –

Love pinned me fast, and I could not resist:
Her ghostly nails were driven through each wrist.

FINBARR AND THE SERPENT OF GOUGANE BARRA

Did it exist?
                    For hours I'd scan the surface
Hope for a splash, a shadow in the water,
Anything
            to puncture the mysterious.

At night I'd set the traps with squeaking bait.
But nothing came
                    except a badger and an otter.
Yet still I felt its presence by the lake.

At last, I snapped: I drove the serpent out
With curses, shouts — I exorcised the beast
Along with every slithery scaly thought.

But soon… I could not bear the certainty
Of absence, emptiness.
                        I headed east
To settle where the plains of marshes lie

And built a trap, a cave-like oratory;
And here I pray for god
                    to coil around me.

THE MONASTIC
STAR-TIMETABLE

"On the holy night of Christmas
When you see the Dragon above the dormitory
And Orion poised above the chapel roof
Prepare yourself to sound the bell."

Darkness freezes round me in the cloister.
The vellum words and stars inflict their patterns
Whispering like the ceaseless prayers we send to God.
No one must lie asleep who must protect the world.

"On the festival of Saint Germanus
Look for the jewel of the Archer's arrow
Hanging above the middle of the tower:
That is when to start the night-time hymns."

The stars are our seasons, the keys of our prison:
Winter snowfall, glitterings of spring rain
The globes of poppies in the harvest fields
The dying meteors of copper beech, oak and elder.

"On the Lord's circumcision
When the bright star in the knee of Artophilax
Is level with the corner of the dormitory
It is time to bring the taper to the lamps."

The thrill of live flame! A writhing spirit,
The chapel like a soul skinned with gold,
This is the light I seek beyond the constellations;
O *lux aeterna*, burn off my crusted life!

"On the feast of our beloved Saint Agnes
When you see the Virgin's spears rising clear
Above the space between the sixth and seventh windows
Make ready for the sacred office."

I dread nights of fog, mist, vapours, cloud
The clinging absence, the separation from God.
Lord, how long before a star expands inside me
Flooding my soul and flesh with gracious light?

"On the feast day of Saint Clement
Orion will rise above the end of the refectory –
But wait until you see the sword and scabbard
Before you wake the brethren."

So many nights I've waited for eternity
Listening for music, looking for meaning,
But all I've felt is the dark between the stars,
My heart, beating like a bell, the phrases of mortality.

MAGNA KARISTIA

I leave parchment to continue this work, if perchance any man survive and any of the race of Adam escape this pestilence and carry on the work which I have begun.

Friar John Clyn, *Kilkenny, 1349*

Lord, your work is now reversed.
No cockcrows spit the bloody dawn
Wheat whispers like fields of glittering wasps
The fruits of orchards hang down
Fat and untested ... we crumble to the dust
From which we were once born.

How can all this dying bring redemption?
How will you burn us into angels
With skin of gold of the light of sun
From blackened bodies dumped in wells?
Forgive my doubts of heaven
Amid the sweet miasma of this hell.

Who will survive to shoot memories
From age to age like swallows
Joining distant countries?
Who will preserve fire, earth, snow
The first green shivering of trees
The flow of pilgrims to the Barrow?

The reason that you made us –
Surely – was to witness your creation?
Without us what will be your purpose
As you walk around your garden
In eardrum-silence, echoes
Of the hooves of Death spreading on

And on – each night my sleep is beating
Over what my being has amounted to
Beyond cold vigils, chanting
The isolation of beatitude
Always giving thanks and never doubting
Why so much of it was due.

I gave my youth to find your paradise
Within this cell and cloister
Now every little sacrifice
Flares and rages – has stripped me to a pair
Of jittery fiery eyes
Skidding off corpses everywhere.

Lord, for years I have been dying
Leeched white by sterile days,
Lacklustre nights; instead of trying
To exorcise the haze
Of tepid piety – instead of crying
Out for grace, I mouthed your praise

While desperate to feel your fire in me,
Yet dreaded it, resisted till the kiss
Of apathy
Or warm embrace of fickleness
Would welcome my return to the
Familiar chapel of my emptiness.

You could have driven me pure
Transfigured me with light – one vision
Just one! would have made me sure
This life of yours was really mine.
Each day, like a dog, I waited for
Your unmistakeable sign

And now it comes – as flaming blood
Distilling fear to keener fear
And no escape; no ark bobs on the flood
Of this fetid waveless atmosphere –
The dark age has come – God
Deliver me, prepare

My soul … the world's light darkens,
The future tunnels to the past.
This blank paper is my afterlife, a token
Of the hope I've lost.
Lord start again. Make the earth
Afresh from this

Great Dearth

VERBUM

from "Kells"

"Remember this.
I do not have a name or face, or form,
and words and paint prolong the lie
that I can be depicted: I am beyond
all sense of what 'beyond' can mean.
To know me, close your eyes
and leave the road of affirmation,
the road of thinking and imagining:
just be a pilgrim to yourself,
alert, not knowing where to go,
but trusting in your ignorance
and travelling inward all the time.
Observe the spirals of your thoughts,
the interlace of hopes and fears
feeding off each other endlessly;
watch circles of your good intentions
revolving ineffectually,
the circles of jealousy and resentment –
just watch your convoluting self
proliferate without your intervening
until it dies away to nothing
but silence, a perfect stillness.
And if you bear the beautiful eeriness
of being aware without your I,
then home may come to you
as you surrender everything familiar,
a dispatching you tenaciously resist
because it feels like dying –
waiting for the other to come,

the initial lightening of atmosphere,
the shift, thoughts evaporating
as your sense of self's disabled,
the glow of uncentred awareness –
a crack
a flood of light engulfing
your being, infusing you with love –
if then you see me you've become
the unstained love you sought in me –
then who is who?
The eyes through which you see are mine."

THE SONG OF RICHARD ROLLE

In thinning winter cloud the sun
Finds petals of a Yorkshire rose;
The chapel light softens the stone
Around his knees and calloused toes

And he is deep in holy fire –
Although his nose and fingers freeze
His heart's a furnace and transforms
His godly thoughts to melodies

Of such a sweetness he's impelled
To sing full-chested, eyes shut tight,
Propelling songs to paradise –
Cascades of them – so loud they might

Drown out the angels, wake the saints
As on the last day; yet these psalms
Which shake the galleries of heaven
Lie silent in his prayer-pressed palms.

ANGELS AND HARVESTERS

As thoughts arrive
From god knows where,
Or sun breaks through
A fraying cloud
Emboldening a patch
Of trees, or grass,
They just appeared
From nowhere
Among the harvesters
The field a world
Of cutting, gathering,
Cutting, gathering.
Their outlines sometimes
Flickering brighter,
They walked between
The bending figures
Curious
Pausing to watch,
Like ancestors
Almost remembering
The world they'd left,
Or foreigners
Amused to see
The same things done.
They moved around
Unseen by all –
Unless one glimpsed,
Perhaps, light thicken,
A glassy movement,
As air can wobble

On summer days.
And then they went
Walked into nothing
Just left the world
Without ceremony
Unless it was
The swish of scythes
The swish of scythes

THE PRAM PUSHER'S TALE

I stop and let a car career and swerve,
Continue bobbling the pram down the road
Anticipating bends, switching sides
To escape a sudden silent vehicle
Until relief! I turn off down a lane
Which opens up with trees on either flank;
A spine of grass, weeds, moss divides
The crumbly putty-coloured surface,
With its shadow play of shifting leaves.
Banks melt and spray their beggars' arms
Of briars, dusty blackberries.
I pause before the effort of the climb.

Looking down, I watch her watching eyes,
Bemused and focusing, the tiny lashes flickering.
Amazed by light and god knows what,
She is speechless, receiving messages –
Her eyes are ears, listening
To outer space or some forgotten land
Puzzled, as if a déjà vu were fading like a dream;
And in her eyes I can almost see the trees
Above, their veterans' medals struck by sun
Their branches tasselling gaps of light.

Stationary but moving
There's nothing she can do but look,
Receive the light and wonder at the wonder,
The fluent universe of colours;
For everything flows

In shapes and textures, shades and brilliance
Which have no names, significance.
*
In her I see myself as I am not –
Wonderless, searching more haphazardly
For meaning the more the years slip by
Half fearing some diabolic paradox
That the truth I hope to find
Cannot be found by searching
But only stumbled on by accident
Or granted freely, if at all,
But that I cannot know this
Until I have searched until dementia.
My will impels me, impelled in turn
By a memory of timelessness
A blessèd opening to another world,
A moment many years ago
Which left me helpless as a baby.

Incapacitated, confined to bed
I felt the past squirm up beneath me
A litany of unoriginal sins
More damaged pride than anything
But crippling in intensity.
Then after time, in meditation, prayer
Accompanied by gentle breathing
A crisis of remembering would pass
And there might come a sense of peace
The rip-cord of a parachute released
Silkily, floating through my being.

Each day the pattern would repeat itself:
The breathing loosening the body
An ebb and flow, ebb and flow
That led to subtle shifts of lightness;
Then stronger moments of expansion
Would lift and soften consciousness,
Erase incoming scatterings of thought
And bring about a silence,
A sphere without a boundary
Without a centre.
The sense of being sharpened, purified,
Of sympathy awakening
In measure with the fading of the self.

Day after day the peace intensified
Until one morning
My body started losing its solidity
My mind its thought – as usual,
The peacefulness pulsed in
With sudden starts like electric shocks
But too serene, soft-edged to be a shock
And still the peace kept coming on,
Implosions of graduated lightness
Deepening the space of the interior
Pushing its outer edge beyond control
And nothing could be done,
My disappearing self
Could only marvel at the process;
Then it happened –
The splintering of mental membrane
And flesh dissolving – a flash
A wave, atomic blinding

The ingress of obliteration
No inside or outside
A drowning in radiance
As if a holy presence had descended
And found an emptiness it had to flood,
There was no me, no thought, no body
Just new-born helplessness;
And simultaneously my heart released
A joy that blossomed uncontrollably
So physical, tingling, undirected,
Circulating in veins of light
As if the sun, risen in my core,
Had unified creation
And I was that creation.

And then it ended.

The self I thought had disappeared returned.
Although there'd been no thought, no body,
My mindlessness it seems still harboured
A minuscule materialising fear –
Despite the overflowing joy –
The fear that if I had no me
I would disintegrate, go mad, or die,
So something stirred, and forced me back to earth.

A reservoir of peacefulness remained
For days, for weeks, leaking drip by drip
A living presence which became a memory
Receding like the letters on a gravestone
A hungry ghost demanding to be fed
The light again, just as it was,

Complaining at the lack of silence
The tumbling in of hopes and fears
Dismays and pleasures, listlessness,
On which it fed like blood.
*

Decades have passed. I have another self
A pramful of anxieties
A source of love as well –
She is amazed by everything
Which passes overhead:
The flotsam of the moulting trees
Serrated silhouettes of crows
A sky without horizons.
Pusher and pushed, slow-moving comet,
She the cone and I the tail,
Snailing around this undulating circuit
All circumference and no centre
We pass familiar constellations:
The village pub and post office, the old grey church,
The yard with the dilapidated van
The road with overhanging trees
The glebe lands and the graveyard –
I've come to know exactly when
To cross the road or dodge a rut or pot-hole
To tip the pram to counteract the camber.
Each daily round's a layer of my life
Peeled off, irrevocably lost,
I leave the house and come back just the same
Indifferent to the fields and trees and sky
Insensible to anything but random thoughts
But haunted by light, and by her face
Deep limestone eyes

Searching into space like mine
Almost remembering paradise.

THE PERSEIDS

(August 2017)

On the plateau of Bosmenditte
we watched the sky deepen
and the last Pyrenean peaks
creeping from the bronze age,
the six of us on the grass,
two lots of parents, two daughters,
assembling chairs and a table,
foraging for rotted twists of oak
to make a fire, a token of the dying sun.
We broke bread on top of the world,
poured red wine into mugs,
and alternated between
the pitter-patter of conversation
and listening to the rhythm
of clonking bells: a group of cows
had gathered by the slope's edge,
watching us with moon-eyes,
their bodies cream-white.
And from a nearby tor
a dozen sheep ambled down,
approached the cows and stopped
like stationary clouds, glowing
in the still-darkening sky, our fire
the sole flickering of movement.
Until a movement on the road
between bushes – a horse galloping,
then five more, dark brown and tan,
their manes flowing like mantillas –

they halted opposite the cows
and sheep, and joined the vigil.

We lay on rugs on spongy moss
huddled for warmth, heads on stomachs,
our prayers and wishes at the ready.
And nothing came.
The animals entered dark outlines
and constellations marked the bones
of giant mythic beasts and beings,
Cassiopeia and Ursa Major,
Pegasus, Cygnus the Swan.
And still we waited, with nerves
and hearts as much as eyes,
as if we were waiting for new lives
to open up miraculously
or some spark to jolt us
into different ways of thinking.
And as we wondered, "Will they ever come?"
three of us shouted, the others
exclaiming "Where? Where?" –
we pointed to the interstellar spaces
and there, a streak of light, a cry of wonder,
then a rush of thicker light, its wake
fizzing like a rocket's tail,
a smaller star unzipping a patch of dark.
And on they came, popping up,
as slight as blinks
or like torches of white fire
drawn across the immensity of space –
as if a veil had fallen
and we were watching

the stirrings of the universal mind,
each cell and synapse and signal
in the firmament of its being.
Up our wishes flew, and prayers, too,
our backs moulded in the mountain top
our eyes filling with endlessness.

And in the freckled darkness
the stars looked down on us
and on the gathering of silent animals,
as if they'd willed us there, the ones
they had been waiting for,
ensouling the universe
with our thoughts for sick and absent friends
and wishes for uncertain futures –
the stars saw the meaning of life –
if only for the time it took
to see and lose a prayer
in our evaporating trails of love.

SERAPHIM OF SAROV

(After a conversation between Nicholas Motovilov and Seraphim in November 1831)

The day was born in twilight,
grey above the forest glade,
the earth deepening with snow
as snow kept falling from the sky;
the fields pure white below the hill
beside the River Sarovka.
I sat on a stump opposite him;
all I could smell was fir trees.
"The only thing in life," he said,
"is to make ourselves a home
to welcome the holy spirit.
Nothing more. All else will follow.
Our souls use words for prayer,
but when the spirit descends
we must stay silent ..."
I glanced at him: imagine
staring at the centre of the sun
and there you see someone's face,
lips moving, eyes expressive,
and you hear a voice speaking,
feel your shoulders being held
by hands you cannot see;
in fact you do not even see yourself,
just a dazzling light, diffusing
and making the glade luminous
and the snowflakes layering the snow.
I felt such peace in my soul;

no words could express it.
And such warmth.
No words can express it.

THE FACE

(Icon of Christ the Redeemer, Andrei Rublev, Tretyakov Gallery)

I turned a corner and saw your eyes
as if *you* had turned a corner
in the moonlight of a deserted city
and seen me looking in surprise
at the faded colours
of your disembodied, floating face.
I wanted to touch it
like the woman daring to touch the edge
of your robe to heal herself.

I want to touch that moment again
before the wood reclaims you
forever, withdraws you into its grain,
your features too unearthly,
too full of light for this world,
assaulted by the stares of believers
and unbelievers, erasing you
second by second, day by day,
with too much hope, or idle curiosity.

TRINITY

(Icon of the Trinity, Andrei Rublev, Tretyakov Gallery)

We had gone to Moscow on a journey
from the suburbs of Dublin
and scattered townlands of West Cork,
flying eastward into darkness,
a night of prehistoric stars,
millennia of Christianity evolved
in our names: Joseph, John and James.
And then we came, at last, to stand
in timelessness before our heritage,
forgetful of belief and unbelief.
We had the icon to ourselves,
like three angels, invisible, or making
the crowds in the gallery invisible;
conforming to a gentle communion,
sharing thoughts, bits of knowledge,
subsiding to colour, inherent gold,
the inner circularity of the tableau,
we felt our selves dissolving ...
three strangers in the desert of Mamre,
sharing the freedom of wanderers
rejoicing in the chance events
and small miracles of life –
an oak tree spreading out its shade,
a little water, morsels of bread –
and snatches of words and sounds
that stir to life the unpredictable:
the whispers of Abraham at his tent,
Sarah's mocking gasp of laughter –

the prospect of a birth,
two becoming three,
three becoming one.

from VACANAS

When I listen for you in the creak of a door
Or wind at the window, my mind chatters
Like martins making nests beneath the eaves;
And all I hear is gabbled garble
Expressing everything about nothing.

Let me retreat from noise
And be the silence of my waiting.

*

I want to love this ancient church,
The eagle lectern, snowy altar cloth,
Beams of oak and angels lit in glass.
Then I look outside the porch door
And see you strolling down a lane towards the stream.

Bring the inside out, the outside in.

*

The earth cannot contain its holiness:
Snowdrops hold vigils in the frost
Bluebells sway on pilgrimage in woods
Kingcups raise chalices by rivers
And roses hear confessions from bees.

Teach me a gentle tread
And let my eyes see kindly.

THE CHURCH OF AIR

I enter the nave as if walking through
A closed door, dissolving the material;
My every thought's a blink of an eye
Or imperceptible dilating pupil –
Suddenly I'm walking through a memory,
A summer on the root-buckled road
From ancient Wilton to Stratford Tony
Old beech trees vaulting either side –
Branches touch like prayerful fingers
As if they're trying to close a crack
In Creation by weaving leaves together,
Like emerald feathers on an Aztec cloak.

The nave of air stretches for as long
As the mind can imagine; the transepts
Are the garden of Reagh on Sliabh Bawn;
The left has the arch of the box hedge
That leads you to a *hortus conclusus*
Of dew-glinting grass, wild roses in trees,
A green bench, and beds of asparagus.
The right reveals the Reagh Maze
With hedges of hawthorn and yew – I enter
The path, like a memory of my life,
And wind towards the hazel at the centre
From which I pluck a golden leaf.
Between the transepts, the crossing floor
Is the grassy gravel of Reagh's drive
Where my sister's creaking tortoise crawls
Towards a glowing cucumber slice –

Dear Zoë, dear Life, half blind,
Drowned in a puddle and placed in a grave
But later unearthed by chance, you crept
Blinkingly, like Lazarus from his cave.

The choir is my April garden at home
In the hill-top hamlet of Rossmore
And swallows are flitting to and from
The darkness of the shed's open door
With twigs for nests – their tails flick
Like the slick batons of conductors
As they sing out strings of click-music
Imbibed from the insects of Africa.
Behind the shed a wren in the furze
Is thrilling full of life, and a crow
Up above – a rag of black sky – flies
From Murphy's field to Lyre Cross.

The altar is our square kitchen table
With tartan cloth, candle and clutter
The envelope of an unpaid bill
A tumbler and postcard from Padua –
Tools for putting out a bee or wasp;
And the kitchen wall is the reredos
With my daughter's paintings – a lighthouse
And a lemon of waxy lemon-ness.
Or the altar is the tree-cradled rock
That lies there long and sleek in the field
Beyond our house and the spruce stacks –
A haven where, on the trudge up hill
Through wet salaams of grass,

I shelter from sun or blinding rain
And still myself, like Brendan, motionless
On the back of a pumice-smooth whale.

And as I glide through this airy church
I murmur confessions to myself
Of sins and faults of the sort that lurk
And wait for moments of unguardedness;
But this time – I forgive myself forever!
Obliterating every regret and sorrow.
And as I move, unencumbered,
I mingle with like-minded souls or those
Who've stumbled in, unsure where they are
And wondering what happens next
Then realise, amazed, that they are *here*
And there is no "then", "now" or "next".
And all the while, music's in the air,
The song of the blackbird I hear at dawn
Below my window, when light appears
Alleviating the dark of the curtain:
In the glowing screen of benevolence
My fear of sleep, of death, recedes
With the bird's unfollowable sequence
Of flutings – breath at its sweetest.

And prayers first of all recall
The utter strangeness of existence
The mysteria, the unexplainables
Of love, beauty and coincidence –
As when one time in holiday Kerry
My father drove back to the beach

To look for the tooth he'd lost at sea
Deaf to our churlish doubting jeers;
And, lo!, he found his tooth beneath
A shell, like the pearl of great price.
Then prayers enter the Silence
A common quietude, and we try
To touch the lives of the sick and infirm
By holding their images in mind
To cradle them with the glow of a candle flame
Not knowing if our prayers will succeed
But knowing we're changing ourselves
Just for a moment, and during that moment
We ripple a wave of light to caress
And brighten the aura of the intended.

For the host there's a china tureen
Of my mother's watercress soup –
The cress always cut from the nearby stream
The pot always steaming the kitchen up
As we arrived after driving from London
Our eyes attuned to darkening Wiltshire
The heron-grey liths of Stonehenge
And the distant cone of Salisbury's spire.
The soup my mother kept in the freezer
Where after she was buried it stayed
In scrawled-on cartons by packets of peas
Daring us to thaw her memory away.

And giving the sermon ... is Gautama the Buddha –
The one when he faced a crowd of followers
And finding no word could utter the wordless
He lifted up a lotus flower

And with his smile in bloom he offered it –
Because just then, *it* was the universe,
And one single word might destroy it;
And his smile flowed through them like a wave.

And for the final blessing I can hear
A whisper of Plotinus reminding me
That "our country whence we came is *there*
But we cannot reach it on foot, for our feet
Take us only to realms of *this* world.
Let everything go, shut your eyes
And a way of seeing will unfold
That everyone has, but few of us use".

And as I leave this fading church
And enter wherever my no-self imagines –
I pass through the Romanesque arch
Of Killeshin and gaze from its hilltop ruins
At the fields of Laois and Timahoe's tower
And the church where my granddad Thomas
Is lighting red candles on the altar
Rehearsing his sermon for Evensong.

And leaving the door made of air
There's no priest to pump my hand
But my mother, waiting there,
Looking out for me, ready for a hug
As if I've just returned from school
Aflush with the prospect of summer ahead;
There, too, my dad – with that smile
When I'd open his door and see him in bed

Sunk among corpses of pillows
His smile like a wide-open door –
As if he thought it was a miracle
That I had bothered to visit at all.

And now I pass from home to home
With the joy that Kazantzakis felt
When he wrote what's engraved on his tomb
on top of Heracleion's Venetian wall
among the palms and winter jasmine:
I do not hope for anything
I do not fear anything
I am free

With the joy and simplicity I glimpse
When walking the fields with Cooper our dog
Who's running after ghosts of rabbits
Then dashing back through forest and bog
To check I exist – we're bound together
As we move from dark ranks of spruce
To the sunlit roll of fields and hedges
And Coopy's Labrador-Collie nose
Is sniffing a thousand smells at once –
As if he can smell all the scents of the universe –
And as we move towards the fields beyond
He's a black streak above tips of grass
Dashing to the stream, the banks of gorse
Dashing just for fun
The simple joy of the dash and pause
And dash –

         amen.

POETRY, GOD AND
THE IMAGINATION:
A DIALOGUE

In 2018 John F. Deane and James Harpur began an informal email exchange that explored the relationship between the divine and people and nature. During this correspondence both poets revealed aspects of their abiding metaphysical concerns and tenets, as well as some background to their own work. The dialogue is reproduced here as an introduction and complement to their poems.

James Harpur: John, in our poetry we both explore "God" or at least a divine ultimate truth at a time when Western society has by and large lost its fascination for religion? If there is a God, surely he or she or it has planted a religious or spiritual instinct in us, somewhere. If that is the case how is it manifesting itself? Is there a buried spiritual thirst?

John F. Deane: It appears to me that the "traditional" religious tenets and activities have lost their hold, more or less everywhere. There have been disastrous scandals, abuse, and an ongoing male-fortress mentality in the Catholic Church, but most of all I believe it is a Christian failure to incorporate the reality of evolution and its consequences, that has alienated thinking people. The notion of change appears to be anathema to the Vatican, though not to Pope Francis. Western society has rejected the transcendent for the immediate and corporeal. I believe, and have experienced many times, that people have now an even greater thirst for spiritual things, but have little real guidance in which they can place their trust. "Religious" poetry has always been somewhat denigrated. Our task remains to write good poetry and, if it's one's instinct, to write good religious poetry.

JH: I'm interested that you think it's evolution that's central to Christianity's failure, and maybe you might expand on that. For me, it's more the churches becoming organizational structures. I think of the origins of the church – the first fishermen, the lowly band of peasants and artisans trailing around with Jesus, the first "house" churches, the memories of the actual person of Jesus still lingering, his words still warm from his mouth – loving one's neighbour, embracing the outcasts, etc; and then I think of the great edifices that have evolved, material and conceptual, and the complex theologies that sometimes can be understood only by professional theologians ... and I scratch my head and wonder how we got here. You say, "Western society has rejected the transcendent for the immediate and corporeal", and I wonder whether modern versions of some of our churches in the West have done this as well? The post-Enlightenment emphasis on reason, and the rise of science is necessarily antipathetic to revelations that cannot be explained and is generally sceptical about any source of intuition or inspiration that cannot be accounted for unless it's down to overactive brain circuitry. If religion is anything at all, it is rooted in mystery, epiphany and personal experience, and that's what it shares with poetry. I chuckle at the Anglican bishop Joseph Butler telling John Wesley that his claim of receiving "extraordinary revelations" was a "horrid thing, a very horrid thing!" What would he have made of Blake, Yeats and Hughes? That is to say, poets, who hold the Muse, or the idea of the Muse, as central to their work. But I'm not sure religious poetry has always been denigrated – I would say only in modernist or post-modernist times (yet one thinks of Eliot; and Ted Hughes was the most religious of poets, of a sort).

JFD: To accept evolution is inevitably to deny the doctrine of "original sin" and even that of the "Immaculate Conception". The teaching (Augustine originally) that we are all born tainted by the sin of Adam, brought a feeling of guilt and a fear of relishing the earth on which we live. This, in turn, brought a fear of the real world, and emphasised the ideas of penance, punishment, sexual sin. I agree with you that a failure to trust the feminine (and there was poor Eve, blamed for it all) impoverished scholastic thinking. The notions behind my own efforts at poetry – apart from working on language, technique, etc – would be an attempt to redeem the language of faith in a wholly acceptable material world in which humanity and the entire cosmos moves towards a completion, a unity, a one-ness with the divinity. I am regaled by Teilhard de Chardin, and a devoted follower.

JH: I like de Chardin too, though I do wonder whether he's right in positing that we, the human race, are in spiritual evolution. Looking at some of our present-day politicians and other grand folk one might think the opposite. I like your mission to redeem the language of faith, but does that boil down to investing nature with spiritual values, or trying to make words such as *spirit, soul, mass, host, incarnation,* more meaningful? For myself,

I tend, perhaps from early Classical influences at school and university, to be a Golden Ager, namely that we're passing through successive phases of degenerating civilization. I think you may be more spiritually optimistic than I am, and have more faith in the traditional structure of Christianity and perhaps other religions (though I know you harbour great reservations about the former). Would that be fair?

JFD: All that is fair; for me Teilhard de Chardin sees humanity as the leader in spiritual evolution, not that we have evolved in that area to a wondrous extent! That's our task, and for me Christianity – when it means following the example of Christ, and not the tenets of any given Church – is the way such progress must be made. I think we are not really doomed to dream backwards, in our time, but we are going through a transitional phase and a radical change is necessary. Interesting to read in today's *Irish Times* (12 Jan, 2018) the words of Archbishop Martin: "We're in *Titanic* country, so there's no point replicating past strategies that have clearly failed. Radical change is the only serious option now and with Pope Francis pointing the way we need bishops who are prepared to follow his lead in taking a fresh and radical change of direction." Hard to see the stuck-in-the-male-fortress Vatican gang move like that.

In poetry, I believe a fairly radical approach is also needed; too much of contemporary poetry, for me, seems vapid and imitative, saying nothing and saying it well. Your own way of telling a story that moves from personal experience outwards, through events both small and cosmic, seems to me to be radically different and effective; your Kells work, for instance, your comets, your silhouettes… all engaging and yet carrying profound truths. Poetry should strike the heart more often, as yours does, and not simply the bookshelves and idle fancy. I think the notion of

Golden Ages has disappeared down a mine-shaft and we will be lucky to survive our modern age in any way we can!

JH: Enjoyed reading that quote from Archbishop Martin! I've come to the opinion, via the spiritual thinker J. Krishnamurti, that organizations kill the thing they try to promote, no matter how virtuous or saintly the thing. For me the churches are "anti-Christ" – not in a Book of Revelation way, but simply anti what Jesus was saying, namely that the life of the spirit is about being compassionate and not being in thrall to abstractions such as *spirit, transcendence, immanence, original sin, immaculate conception.* Re poetry, I have always thought that it was in service to the investigation of the great mysteries of life – love, death, time, nature – and their interrelationship, as well as the divine. I think this comes partly from my early exposure to those great sacred epics, the *Odyssey* and *Aeneid*, and partly my upbringing with its variety of spiritual sources. The Harpurs have had Church of Ireland ministers for generations, and my mother was an enthusiast of, shall we say, a more "Yeatsian" esoteric spirituality. More than that, she went to a Quaker school and imbibed the Friends' ethos; she was famous for driving in the middle of country lanes to avoid killing wildlife on the margins! I have found myself more and more becoming Quakeresque – pacifist, vegan; "everything that lives is holy", as Blake said. *But* perhaps writing poems about shopping in Asda or losing one's iPhone is more natural, more humble, more earthly, and more Zen?

JFD: Yes, and it has always amazed me how the churches got it wrong: the scriptures seem clear and the churches twisted them to suit their own ends. Love is what it's all about and the Vatican in particular appears to me to run away from that word. The Catholic Church has influenced all I do, including the poetry;

I was brought up in its most authoritative seasons and it took me years, and four of those in a seminary, to find out that – in there – it was not love that was the source and end, but the institution itself. I like to think of the poetry as issuing out of the foul rag-and-bone-shop of the heart, but also out of the pure-snow loving of the spirit. I was never told how to take the Spirit (that wee bird of the gospels that becomes a fire of love and service at Pentecost) but now I see a route from the mud through prayer into the transcendent, and that prayer as laying oneself open to the suggestions of the Spirit, after the experiences, the thought, the reading have been done. So, the poem occurs where the reason hits the blank wall, and the imagination takes one glidingly through to the other side. And this, I insist, may well be shopping at Asda, as well as wrestling with the angel at the edge of the great ocean.

JH: You speak of "prayer into the transcendent": who, may I ask, do you pray to? What image do you have of the object of your prayer? Are your poems prayers in disguise? Don't dodge the first two questions!

JFD: Oh dear ... I move about a great deal amongst the influential ones! My truest prayer, if I have any, is to Christ: "Amen, amen, oh Christ, my Christ, Amen!", an acceptance of the action of Christ in my spirit. So, to Jesus Christ, whom I work to know and love as well as I can. Otherwise: to the Trinity, Father, Son and Spirit, and recently more so to the Spirit, the feminine, inspirational, gifting side of God. And to Mary: I was born on 8 December and have always had a warm devotion to her, re-cently – and for very real and extraordinary reasons – to Mary as portrayed in Guadalupe Mexico; also, from childhood, to Mary of Knock ... always now to Mary as Mother, not as the

"Virgin Mary". Then I pray to and for and with those I have loved and lost in death over the years, closest perhaps to my brother Declan whom I feel sometimes beside me, and to my godmother Patricia who died when I was just a few months old but whose being moves in a realm where I feel myself concerned. Do not ask me to elucidate further: it's something that cannot be pinned down. And I do believe in prayer (though Mayo has *not* won the all-Ireland football championship – yet Ireland has done pretty well in rugby!): not necessarily asking for stuff, but hoping to come closer to the eternal Wonder. Now, no dodging there; so, how about you? I see my poems not as prayers, nor vice versa, but the poems are results of prayer sometimes, and the best work, even phrases and words, seem to be gifted, rarely, but often enough to make me pause and think … and be grateful.

JH: I like the way you have a team of characters to pray to – and I remember we both pray to our fathers for a parking space! I suppose what interests me is the image we have of "God". I'm agnostic – in the proper sense – about God, and I don't want to get into Meister Eckhart's "we must get to the God behind God", but … if I were to pray to "him" I would probably fall back on an image of an old man in a long white robe. Yes, seriously. Probably because of the repetition of "Father" in the NT and traditional iconography. I know that image has been shot out of the waters long ago. But when we pray, unless it's a silent prayer, or the Jesus Prayer, and God is involved, don't we have to have an image? Otherwise God might easily resemble the Neo-Platonic *One*, that impersonal fountain of continual light – wasn't it the strength of Christianity to emphasise a relationship with a divine being that was more personal than that?

In a similar vein, poets have traditionally prayed to the Muse for inspiration – usually a divine female figure. Is praying to the Muse the same as praying to "God", and why not just pray to God for inspiration, cut out the middle woman? After all, as a good puritan, Milton invokes the Holy Spirit in *Paradise Lost* as his Muse. Even if I don't pray consciously to a Muse, I believe in the effect of the Muse, the process of the Muse: namely waiting for the thought, the feeling, the synchronistic clash of inner and outer worlds to happen; this can mean a long wait – I haven't written for years. But I think your process is different – are you more in touch with a Muse? Can you direct her to me?

JFD: I have no image of God as Father: so I rely on a multi-construct Christ figure, but mostly I simply try to focus on my own interior silence where I trust God waits. My Muse is also a construct: from readings, notes, trial bits and pieces, and then a prayer to the Spirit (so, to God direct) and a slow effort at writing, waiting, trying to listen. Sometimes it works, or appears to. But I keep writing as I try and set up a theme, or a particular sequence of events or images and try to keep one piece leap-frogging over another. If I don't keep something moving all the time, nothing for me would ever happen; so I have endless notebooks of drafts and failures and out of each notebook might emerge three or four pieces. Currently, for instance, my theme is sight: I have worried all my life about becoming blind. Now I support Sightsavers with cash; I am working on a piece about the life of someone on Achill who gradually did grow blind and who asked me to come and read from Longfellow for her. The breadth and width of the notion of sight urges me in all sorts of directions, out of which nothing really valid has come as yet, but there are the usual trills and frolics. So I keep labouring at the compost heap, hoping to see a shoot somewhere! I would like to have the Holy Spirit as Muse: and I have a long poem done about exactly that, "By-

The-Wind-Sailor", a fanciful piece with which I'm reasonably pleased. My talk on Yeats for the Temenos Academy will lead up to the Spirit as Muse, though Yeats would have, and did have, other names for that ... Milton's particular Holy Spirit would not work for me, as I think God, too, evolves, or at least does so in our eyes as we evolve. Housemaid's knee was something I suffered from when I was in the seminary: praying too much on my knees: now I try centering prayer (often dozing off as I do it in a very comfortable chair) and, of course, the Jesus prayer. I may yet write that poem I'm supposed to; and you will, too.

JH: That's a nice thought you end with, though I fear this: every poem we write on earth is merely a rehearsal for the poem we would write in the afterlife, except on reaching the latter we will find we no longer find the need to write it. I'm still curious, though, about your relationship to "God": you say you have no image of God, and yet you write as if he/she is a personal divinity. You refer to the interior silence "where I trust *God waits*" and also to making a prayer to the Spirit "(so, *to God direct*)". I'm not trying to catch you out here – it's an area I tussle with; having grown up with the idea of a personal creator, a personal divine entity to which I can pray, confess, confide, I now wonder whether that is delusional. Plotinus, crudely speaking, wrote of a divine dispensation involving a central source of light, emitting light, like a spiritual fountain, and the light taking Forms, from which our everday reality is created; our task in life is to retrace our steps towards the primal light; so, there is a reciprocity of light being emitted and our returning to it. But the Christian objection to Plotinus has been, I think, that the divine process is too impersonal – without a sense of a personal relationship between creator and created. I feel torn; I find it easier to imagine the Neoplatonic process but am loathe to forego a personal relationship with God. And I think this is why I ask people about whether they have an image of God; if you have an image then it makes it easier to have a personal relationship? In Italy recently, I asked an Italian priest and theologian whether he had an image of God. He said (I'm paraphrasing): "I think of God as a child playing on the sand by the sea, a child who is so absorbed in his play that he is unaware of anything else, just being himself in the present time, being full of joy in his play." That struck me. I also recently asked an extremely eminent Anglican theologian the same question and, after a long pause, he said, "Perhaps a chord. A chord of music". I replied: "Can you pray to a chord of music?" I can't remember what he said to that!

I was interested too in your concern about sight, and I wonder whether this is a rational or irrational fear? I'd say everyone worries about going blind, but is there a history in your family of blindness? Given improved treatments and diagnoses the chances of going blind (unless you have a disease) are not that high? What interests me is whether there is a metaphorical implication – fear of loss of vision, i.e. of inspiration, of seeing truth, of imagination, which is something most poets fear, though there's that tradition of the "blind prophet", the physical blindness counterbalanced by visionary intuition, e.g., Tiresias.

JFD: I have been wearing glasses since the age of sixteen and gradually it began to hinder me more and more from playing contact sports, like rugby. Over the years that sight seemed to diminish a little and my spectacles became stronger. I suppose I did fear losing my sight because of all that but recently, an optician told me that my eyesight has improved and I could wear less powerful spectacles. There! the good Ghost moves in strange ways.

I believe that if I don't have the need or ability to write, or even the pen or computer, in the next life, that I shall fall rapidly into despair. I feel low and useless when I am not writing, and feel a little sad when I cannot find a need to tamper with a poem's language or shape any longer; then the temptation is to fling it away or have it published. I think you take far more care and time over your work than I do. I envy that. As to an image of God: I touch on the whole notion of the Trinity, and the sign of the Cross that we Catholics make at the drop of a hat or of holy water. I have hinted that I find the Holy Ghost (I still prefer that word to the Spirit) is a warm and influential presence somewhere in the back-cupboard of my living and I see that Ghost as the breathing of the Father that gave the latter the puff to speak the Word that is the Incarnation. "Glory be to the Father the source and sustenance of our being, to the Son, the spoken name of that source and sustenance, and to the Spirit that gave that naming breath." Amongst all of that the image has to be of Christ, the Incarnate One, whom I have to hold (like the "willing" notion of Boehme) as a real human being and Son of God. Therefore I suppose somewhere in every movement of my spirit towards God, I move towards a real and living person, Christ. The prayer I practise is "centering" prayer, where one tries to avoid all thought and images and simply rest in God; I always find myself trying to stay with a vague image of those who rested in the presence of Christ, like Mary of Bethany and even more so, that poor chap who had the Legion of Devils and who finally came to rest at Christ's feet. So: do you pray in a formal way, with prescribed words, or do you speak to a Presence of some kind? Do you practice any form of contemplative prayer? And do you associate any of that with the writing of your deeply moving poetry? Expand and expound, please.

JH: There's a lot in your last response, both explaining your own practice and asking me about my own, and I feel in harmony with what you say about objects of prayer, especially the sense you convey that it isn't straightforward. I think what concerns me is that those like us brought up in the Christian tradition (you a Catholic, me a nominal Anglican) are used to the idea of a personal God, and I don't just mean incarnate in Jesus but a transcendental figure, not a band of energy, not a fountain of light, not a conglomerate of divine particles which may or may not invest nature. Yet the anthropomorphic figure of God has been jettisoned, I think, at least by the theologians. (But what a wonderful surprise it would be if God did turn out to be like Father Christmas after all.) And I think there is a big divide here, the implications of which have not been addressed, and about which poets might have a say, since we are supposed to be purveyors of the imagination. That is to say that we use the word "God" in general parlance as if he/she/it is a central source of divinity in an anthropomorphic or quasi-anthropomorphic fashion. If I say, "I hope to God the rain stops" or "For God's sake" or "God willing", I'm not referring to a band of energy or Daoist *chi*, am I? Yet when it comes to prayer, the serious business of sending a message to "God" or tuning into him/her/it, the issue of what God is seems more urgent. More than that, what we imagine God to be or not to be should affect our whole metaphysics. If God is a band of energy, say, then it's hard to square it with the message in the New Testament that God sent his only son. Bands of energy don't send sons, nor do "noospheres", pace Teilhard. If Jesus was the son of God, that implies a personal relationship between the two, not someone in Nazareth who has scooped up divine light from an aetherial fountain. That's my area of concern.

With regard to my own praying and so on … re praying for a sick person – I allude to this in my "The Church Made of

Air". Like you I also do a centering meditation, like the Buddhist *vipissana*, on a daily basis, though I often fall asleep. I'm very influenced by the writings of J. Krishnamurti, who suggests a similar sort of meditation, and he uses the phrase "choiceless awareness", i.e., being aware of one's thoughts and feelings, one's jealousies, desires, pleasurable memories, etc., and just *seeing* them, not interacting with them. By "choiceless" he means, I think, that we see without choosing to act or think further on something. When we see a tree our egos or rational minds are usually triggered: "Look, there's a beech tree; it's a big tree; its leaves are turning brown; it's not as nice as the one we saw last year ..." But if we see it choicelessly, we initiate a relationship with the tree without an intervening presence, and in that relationship there is stillness and beauty. Cf. Basho's, "to write about a bamboo you must become the bamboo".

JFD: I feel we are not going to get too far with the theological and rational surveying of the world and of poetry. Without understanding, in an intellectual sense, what the centering prayer does: and what, perhaps, your Krishnamurti is about (though I don't know his work) is letting go of the "false self", the ego that grasps at creation and tries to take advantage of it, enslaves it for the self's own gratification, or simply regards it with love and leaves it as it is. I focus on my efforts at contemplation, centering prayer, by starting with the Trinity: I can sort of deal with the second and third "persons", but the Father remains a cloud of vagueness in my mind. Nowadays that does not bother me; if I can get a hold of God as Trinity, and I can feel the way George Herbert felt towards the Master, Christ, as "my dear" or "Love", then I try and rest in that and let all thought and image flow away from me. I fail often, and I fail well and sometimes, too, I doze off. I think that's all ok ... simply an effort to get beyond the ego and take one's place in a great communion of humanity. Then the Holy Spirit, the shiftless Holy Ghost, without the image of a dove or even a magpie, simply as a guiding Friend, works for me. Twice a day, if I can manage it, I try this for twenty minutes at a time; sometimes, usually, that twenty minutes seems to last an hour and a half; but now and then, rarely, it's a ten-minute thing and leaves me peaceful. The poetry, for me, begins with a very immediate and physical or "natural" seeing, or event, or even memory; I try, when writing the initial stuff down, to let the Holy Spirit take over as much as possible, applying the no-interference approach to the words that come out. Leave it a while, see what I've got, and work on it. All of this is fairly new, and has begun with my efforts at centering prayer, or allowing the Christian (the actual words and work of Christ, and sometimes his presence) to dictate. Hard to do when the world seems aggravating; hard to do also, at the best of times.

In the poetry side of things, directly, I often wonder what your influences have been, in the early days, the middle days, and if you now feel you have some mastery over those influences and are becoming your own true self. It appears to me that in both of your last collections, *Angels and Harvesters* and *The White Silhouette*, you have achieved a singular voice that is very much you and very effective. So how have you come to this point?

JH: To answer your last question re coming to the poetic point I've arrived at, I can only say my means have been muddle, trial and error, and not thinking about "voice" or any sort of trajectory. A sort of tenacious stumbling across a landscape aided by a rare panoramic vista through the trees and occasionally a beam of sunlight hitting me in the face when I'm resting. The very first poem I wrote, at university, for a poetry competition (prize £5!) was about St Patrick getting rid of the snakes in Ireland

— a poem that tried to explore the conflict between spirit and nature. In the poem the snakes simply burrow underground and eat each other to form one gigantic serpent "its back crusted with the hills of Ireland", waiting for "the saints on St Peter's to drop off". I have a feeling that my oeuvre, such as it is, is merely a set of variations on that theme. That eternal tension between spirit and nature, transformed into various guises as the tension between transcendence and immanence, asceticism and world embracement, the *via negativa* and the *via positiva* – this has gripped me for as long as I can remember, mainly because I feel both impulses deeply ("Angels" *and* "Harvesters"!) and I swing from one to the other – in life and art and in aesthetic taste. There's a bit of Hopkins in me – the world charged with the grandeur of God – and there's a bit of Eliot in me, seeking the still point of the turning world.

I don't know why I find the two *via*'s equally compelling and I envy those who have a more unified vision. That's why I cast green eyes at your work – the seemingly unified and inexhaustible celebration of nature in a Franciscan way, the sheer delight in the haecceitas of creation. I know that you have your dark nights of the soul, but the key note in your poems seems to be a massive *positiva*? Am I wrong in this? Do you prefer to keep your black dogs within the sphere of living rather than let them bark in the poems? Or do you alchemically transform darkness into light, as in your pearl of a poem, "Pearl"?

JFD: In your last you say you get inspiration with "occasionally a beam of sunlight hitting me in the face when I'm resting": something I feel is utterly true for, perhaps, most of us. There is a receptivity there, usually quite unconsciously; a restfulness, when the well-nigh impossible works a moment, the task of voiding the mind of thoughts, distractions, emotions, plans, the past, the future ... so leaving the mind open to the "incoming", in whatever form of muse or spirit of prophecy or whatever that incoming may be called. It appears, too, that this passivity is not, in fact, mere passivity; the ground of the mind and spirit has been prepared, by life, by thought, by reading, and by one's earlier efforts. Indeed, as you also suggest, it may simply be another way of saying, or trying to catch, the truths we have come to hold over many, many years, and tried to articulate in many, many poems. And we will never come to the end of that. Dare one call oneself "a poet" until one has finished an oeuvre that is worth looking at; dare one ever call oneself "a Christian" until one has taken upon oneself the full mantle of the Christ. So: can our labour be a method of leaving the mind open, if one can find such a method; and can one have developed a technique to catch and hold the delicate Ariel that is offering the poem? Touching, as you also suggest, the still point of the turning world, or Merton's "point vierge", while at the same time immersing oneself in the tar and mud of everyday actual survival mechanisms? It's a challenge; it's thwarting; it's exhilarating!

There's a new book out that stirs up the soup in the area of Christian thinking that I have laid out in a big bowl before me. It's back to the basic notion of the Christ: that universal Being that was "there" pre-beginnings and that will be "there" post-endings, the Alpha and the Omega; this is the Christ as beside and counterpoint to the physical person of Jesus who stepped out of that mess of being into personhood and took upon himself all that our humanity can and cannot do and suffer. The book is by Richard Rohr and pushes on with the outlines of the faith in and commitment to the Christ that I have outlined in our earlier conversations. I still find it compelling; I find it urges towards a unification of all humankind, all nature, all creation. When they present, on TV, a "picture" of a black hole somewhere in the universe billions and trillions of light years away from us, and of a size and extent vaster than my little mind can even begin to grasp, then am I flummoxed and feel how tiny one little person is in the utterness of things. So, perhaps, these black holes are also in my own psyche, and they are there very close to the surface; it is an act of love and an act of the will at the same time that turns me to the Hopkins task of getting down on my knees to sketch and make present the beauty and wonder of the small things, like the superb loveliness of the scarlet pimpernel surviving on a path newly covered with tarmacadam, of how a mouse-eared chickweed with its tiny and impossibly designed flower can flourish on the cement that holds a high brick wall together. I shudder with apprehension and with delight at the thought of the extent of creation, the cosmos; and I shudder with a certain sadness and a real sense of loss if a fly the size of a pin-head is crushed against a window-pane and leaves the most miniscule drop of blood as a stain upon the cosmos. Out of such positives and negatives, are the black dogs and the chirping poodles of my poems formed. And it all depends greatly on the waiting, the silence; as with Yeats's Caesar, his hand under his head, and "Like a long-legged fly upon the stream, His mind moves upon silence;" that is how he planned his deadly assaults. Then there is Wordsworth with his moving "Tintern Abbey" and "While with an eye made quiet by the power / Of harmony, and the deep power of joy, / We see into the life of things".

JH: I don't know Richard Rohr's work, but from the little you say of him, with the idea of unification of all creation, I was reminded of de Chardin and his exhilarating vision. Which leads me onto … I've always been drawn to daring summations of the divine workings in the human or natural sphere – I'm thinking

of Plato's Forms, Jung's Collective Unsconscious, de Chardin
– but now I'm more sceptical. For thousands of years we have
come up with religious systems and ideals without changing
human nature. That for me is the root problem. Human nature.
The Gospel could not be clearer – love your enemy, sell your
possessions and give them to the poor, be kind, be humble, be
grateful for what you have got, trust that your life will be in
good hands. Human nature in its Christian guise pays lip service to this and then constructs edifices – conceptual, physical
and corporate – that by their very nature emphasise power,
hierarchy and inequality. Human beings seem to be predicated
on the need for power and filling the absence of felt love in
their hearts, the psychic black hole, with material "stuff". All
our endless systems and theories, no matter how uplifting,
haven't changed that. That's why I resonated in particular with
your "sadness and a real sense of loss if a fly the size of a pin-
head is crushed against a window-pane and leaves the most
miniscule drop of blood as a stain upon the cosmos". For me
that is the essence of what we should be; not theorisers or
poets but empathisers; how can anyone who really feels the
death of a fly bear to carry arms against a fellow human being?
All of us should become Jain monks for a day – the ones who
wear masks over their mouths in order not to imbibe insects
and who brush the path in front of them in order not to crush
living creatures. Maybe it's a natural by-product of poetry (and
art) – to inculcate a sense of empathy or to raise consciousness. I'm thinking of Hopkins's plea at the end of "Inversnaid"
("Let there be wildness and wet"); and Larkin accidentally killing
the hedgehog ("We must be kind to each other while there is still
time"). Who would want to build a huge theme park on Achill
Island after your poems have created a deep empathy with its
every nook and cranny and wildness? The way into poetry, and

art, is as you say, the great stillness and silence, though I sense, and perhaps fear, that the extreme edge of silence leads to the Silence that sees art for what it is: part of the expression of the struggle and not the supreme at-ease-ment of unified being.

JFD: What excites me, that stems from Simone Weil, through Teilhard de Chardin and Ilia Delio, is the central figure of the Christ (God enfleshed for a time in Jesus) and how his cross and resurrection is what I see as the ultimate "point vierge" of all of cosmic history and its evolution towards consciousness; Rohr and the "theologians" (though I don't really see him as such, more as interpreter of this developing consciousness), help me to put flesh on the ideas. Yes, I suspect it is possible to see all of this as some new form of theory of utopian (Turkish) delight and I agree that human nature has not changed since Adam sucked on his first soother; and yet, and yet and nevertheless! I have a belief in the Spirit that guides and directs our history and that even the wickedness we are witness to forms part of that necessary dialectical movement: the growth and decay that morphs into new and richer growth. I do not figure that a creator God worth his or her salt, would envision a creation where even those who go against the manifest will of goodness (as we see it, and who can judge?) will be consigned to a muddy end. My optimism grows as I decay myself but there are still many days when the fug of doubt sets in and the heart appears to close over in some sort of hopeless self-preservation.

Of course I agree with you that the Christian message could not be clearer, simpler, and never quite put into practice! But so-called civilisation keeps shifting and all one can hope is that the shift is corrective and in the direction of deeper and more loving consciousness. There are many movements in our time, secular, faith-urged and caring for the environment that offer glimmers of real hope and I have trust in the generation coming after us, in their wisdom, their practical good sense, their active engagement in meaningful causes. Whether or not the scales are weighted in their favour remains to be seen.

What bothers me most is not the seeming failure of Christian values but the insistence of the generality of humankind in the notion of cost-benefit analysis: everything, including poetry, must be subjected to the almost mechanical and soul-less business of value for loot and you and I, who are deeply engaged in activities that – when subjected to a cost-benefit analysis – will come up very short indeed. The problem is that this also appears to apply to the arts in general, to university courses, to anything and everything that is undertaken by human beings. It is the pulse of the huge corporations, of many of the major governments, and has spread right down to the Arts Council of Ireland and the Ministry of Arts and Culture, not only here, but in many other countries. It is still my belief that what you and I and so many others strive after, is a basic need for human fulfilment, and that it is essential that the highest standards in the arts be even more than ever insisted on, and that every effort be made to keep the arts and humanities at the forefront of the human journey. This includes such disciplines as theology, history, geography and so many other subjects currently under threat.

JH: Yes, I quite agree about the reduction of arts and similar concerns to economic utility. In fact with regard to poetry I think it's a heresy, because the implication is that poetry is a predictable nine-to-five job and not a "spiritual" calling. Poetry combines the *un*predictable call of prophecy and the craft of pottery. The starting point for poetry is the incursion of the ineffable, and that's like the oracle at Dodona, where the priestesses would wait for Zeus to speak through the sacred oak tree, through the whisperings of its leaves. The idea that poetry is a trade, a craft (though it requires craft), a skill you chip away at, is behind the creative writing programmes in universities. I don't recall Emily Dickinson or William Blake doing their MA's in creative writing? Conversely, I chuckle when I think of Yeats invoking the moon and putting gemstones under his pillow for several nights in a row and getting a visionary dream (a method that worked for his lovely poem "In the Seven Woods"). There's also a Viking tradition of sleeping on the grave of a dead poet for inspiration; and then there's Caedmon, that Saxon cow-herd receiving poetic inspiration in a dream. These examples show a different way into creation than that now commonly received.

I would like to have your optimism about the evolution of the spirit and Christ as de Chardin's noosphere apex, but I don't! I can't see any evidence for it! Which is not to say it isn't true. But I don't think "Christ", as interpreted by theologians, is the way. Christian theology is so ingrained that it's hard to see the invisible walls it has formed. I don't believe the ingression of the holy spirit in Jesus of Nazareth was *unique*, whereas Christian orthodoxy insists on this; and I find this insistence divisive. It goes against every instinct I have (fomented by Krishnamurti) that whenever we plant our standards on the hill of a religion, a country, a race, or any other tribe, we are automatically being divisive. We erect a barrier – and even porous and amicable barriers can turn toxic very quickly. Every scenario of friction and violence one hears about around the world is centred in divisiveness and tribalism fed by insecure egos – Catholics and Protestants in Northern Ireland, Shiites and Sunnis and Jews and Palestinians in the Middle East, and so on.

The beauty of art, including poetry, is that it transcends all tribalism and division, or should do; the melting pot of the

Imagination has no limit to it, no barriers and invites anything and everything into its warm embrace in order for the strange alchemy of creation to work its magic. Poetry informed by any dogma doesn't work because it insinuates the condition of necessary belief, and that is not the business of poetry. In this regard, I think there is much sympathy between poetry and what Jesus actually said and did; he spent his whole life trying to convince people that "religion" was not about "believing" certain doctrines, but about being loving and inclusive; about not building walls. He embraced lepers, women, tax gatherers – the outcasts of society. He had no ego, he was porous – and for me that is the way.

JFD: That was a rich and direct out-pouring, very much a spirited and spirit-haunted offering. I have relished it. And yes, the whole poetry producing machinery of the universities, workshops and MFA programmes, is often (for there are exceptions) simply pulling the wool over vulnerable people's heads, though many do enjoy the feel of that comforting wool until it falls threadbare. But I think, though poetry and prophecy are near allied in many ways, neither poet nor prophet can merely lurk in the corner of a garden or behind a city wall waiting for the wind to blow the cobwebs away. One must labour to be prepared for what comes, particularly when it comes at the most unexpected times. During the famine times, which are common to us all, when the poetry does not take shape, the spirit works and waits, trial pieces, notes, readings, discussions, translations … all of that labouring will eventually prepare the lines, the pen, the mind, the computer, for the disturbance of the spirit.

I find it hard to directly and heartedly say that I reject my Catholic upbringing, basically because it has given me my life, my hope, my holding. But I have always felt it was another "club" with its rules for playing the game, but of course it is the game itself which matters and where one is basically on one's own, following the course of the ball. Oh dear: I don't want to get carried into the mud-flats with this ... but the ball in this case is the Christ. However, as you say, he cried out not about "religion" but about being loving and inclusive, and most certainly not about building walls. When it comes to faith and to poetry, I have come across a piece that speaks of the ancient "pathway of perception", something discovered when the Dead Sea Scrolls were unearthed. This form of searching appears to have been there among the Essenes, so, before Christ, and well developed. The official word is "epinoia", a knowing that comes through intuition and direct revelation, though what form this latter revelation took is not clear. The opposite way of being is "dianoia", a linear, didactic and logical approach that depends on doctrine and dogma.

This, I think, translates into our time as the new versus the old, the new being a reliance on the movings of wisdom and insight, and the old meaning a reliance on the given, the tried and the used-to-be-trusted. So, the searching for the wisdom of Jesus Christ is of immense value, as opposed to seeing him as a "saviour", who saves us if we follow the laws and dogmas laid down, clearly not by him, but by the Church, or Churches that formulate such doctrines depending on their own structures.

But for me – and I have probably said this already, in like and different terms – Christianity is the "good news" of God's love for us, for all of human-kind. This is not a world-view philosophy or theology, not a theological system or set of moral laws, but a revelation to humankind of the breadth and depth of God's love, to be translated into human loving, living and growth. The great barrier is belief in the resurrection: this makes all the difference, the only thing that defends and underlies all our hope and our reasons for being here. It is the movement towards an acceptance of the faith in Jesus as Son of God, or one with the Trinity of Father Son and Spirit, which remains a unity. (No, don't ask: I don't understand, but I do find I love the notion). From the faith in resurrection comes a full understanding of Jesus and a reason for following him, in word and action, going beyond the norms of human rational measurement. It is an act of the will, such a faith, not of reason, for all of its beauty and wonder remain mysteries and it is only an openness to this and a spirit-given knowledge that can accept and penetrate all of this.

Luckily, all of this idea of love and service and growth does not depend on every individual human being – though it is to be hoped that each person, however depraved or saintly or average, is loved by God and holds the Christ deep within – working for the betterment of humankind. Trumpishness, or Putinism, or Netanyahuishness, or Bolsonaroism … all such negativity on the face of the earth, may well be the catalyst needed for the earth to take that one step backwards to allow it to take two steps forward. This I hope, this I pray for, daily, and I cannot see what else we can do save do to the best of our endeavour what we are able to do in our own lives.

My effort at writing poetry has come to the point where I trust more and more in the "epinoia", the intuition, the direct revelation, since preparation and work towards a poem opens the heart to receive what the deepest caverns of the heart already conceal. And it is this preparation to receive "inspiration", or to learn how to wait and gather movements and moments of understanding and "revelation", that ought to be, but that I know is not, the impetus and groundwork of poetry workshops.

JH: I feel very at home with your "epinoia", or intuition, and also, yes, intuition may well need the fallow period of preparation, the reflecting, meditating, reading, etc., for it to be effective. I also understand your commitment to the "Christ", because it's such a fundamental part not only of your own personal upbringing but also ingrained in our society (Western European and specifically Irish). I wasn't sure whether you thought the "Christ" was unique? For example, how do you feel about Gautama Siddhartha, who became the Buddha, just as Jesus of Nazareth became the Christ? Buddha means "Enlightened One" and Christ means "Anointed One", but both, I suppose are meant to designate special status on the individuals – of supranormal kindness and wisdom. For me, what this suggests is that the ability to be Buddha-like or Christ-like is open to everyone, and this was the great message of Gautama and Jesus. I feel uneasy about seeing either of them as unmatchable one-offs, almost like deities fallen to earth. What they did for me is show a way of living life that honours other human beings and the rest of creation. This, essentially, means a loss of ego – that nub which is the centre of jealousy, envy, resentment, pleasure, loneliness, anger, happiness, depression, self-pity (and so on). That is the problem, and it's why I'm drawn to Krishnamurti, who is the only teacher I know who discusses the loss of ego extensively. Unfortunately, losing one's ego feels as if it's going to be like an *actual, physical death* with a complete severance of attachment, both physical and emotional. In other words to lose one's ego feels like suicide, and very few are prepared to do it.

That's part of my long-running internal debate between writing and the quest for inner peace (or Christian *charis*, or buddhahood); writing almost always, at some point down the line, involves the participation or even active engagement of the ego; and the strengthening or fuelling of the ego is the killing of the path to inner peacefulness. Is it possible to write and be enlightened (peaceful)? My feeling is that if you're enlightened you wouldn't bother to write at all — I can't imagine Jesus or Gautama or Socrates being tucked away somewhere and penning sonnets or haiku.

JFD: Perhaps that's not the way it works at all? Perhaps the ego becomes less egoic if the writing helps to clean it out, to get rid of the dross that sullies the mind and spirit. Perhaps it is the writing it out that displays what the thinking and the living are about and not vice versa — how do I know what I think unless I write it down? The way of prayer is also the way to undermine the ego and in the living of the Christ, that is utterly apparent. And it also appears to me that the attempt at contemplation, in whatever form that takes, is a necessary help to the undoing of the ego if, and this is immensely difficult as you know, we can quieten the mind and listen. . . I believe that it is in the facing up to egoic notions, tendencies and actions that the cleansing through writing may happen and that an attempt to clear any egoic appearance in the work — and I don't mean eschewing the personal experience on which a poem may be based — will result in a poem better suited to an awareness of one's own living.

I often think of Yeats in this context, how he strove all his life to outline the mechanisms of inspiration, following trains of thought that might lead him to continue writing and following on towards the conclusions he had not yet discovered. "The singing masters of my soul" that he researched, these have always intrigued me. And that lovely poem, "The Long-legged Fly" takes three individuals who were central to things he loved and gave them their power through their cultivating of silence: such as Caesar pouring over his maps in his tent, not trusting the advice of others as he plotted his campaigns:

Like a long-legged fly upon the stream
His mind moved upon silence.

So, the following as far as possible of a train of thought
or study, and the standing back and allowing the world outside
to penetrate the hardened egoic skull ... these I feel are the
instruments that are important to the writing process. I have
been, as you know, and hope to continue to be, listening to the
music of Olivier Messiaen and trying to grasp his themes and
the processes of his compositions, while attempting to translate
them into words and how my personal experience and thought
will respond to the music and the translating.

JH: I like the idea of the process of poetry cleansing away the
egoic dross, though I'm not sure that over the years, with all
my commitment to writing, I feel any less egoic. But perhaps
I'm not the best judge. Certainly, the actual moment of creating, of writing, has an un-egoic feel to it through entering the
"sacred trance"; and I guess the same could be said of doing any
absorbing activity, from gardening to doing a jigsaw. Yeats's fly
and Olivier Messiaen seem to me to be fruitful threads leading
to the idea of silence at a deep level, though I keep thinking
of Rumi's alleged notion that the "language of God is silence;
all else is mere translation". Doesn't silence mean silence, not
writing about it or from it? As Laozi said, "he who knows, does
not speak; he who doesn't know, speaks" (and in making this
statement he invalidated his own proposition). Can words ever
really improve on reality – I see a beautiful heron standing on
a rock in the Bandon river, the sweep of the river bank behind
him – isn't that enough? Does my reporting or describing the
scene, no matter how skilful the words, add anything to what
I've seen? Why can't I just be with the scene, then let it go? A bit

like the Tibetan monks who created a beautiful mandala out of coloured sands in the Royal Academy in London – taking days to do it – before tipping the whole lot into the Thames. Isn't it really the process and not the product that matters? Why do we assume or hope, egoically or not, that our creations mean much to anyone but ourselves?

ACKNOWLEDGMENTS

Both authors would like to thank Michael Schmidt and Carcanet Press, as well as Wild Goose Publications, for kindly allowing them to use poems published in the following collections.

John F. Deane: *Toccata and Fugue* (2000): "Penance", "Francis of Assisi 1182 : 1982" and "Christ, with Urban Fox"; *Manhandling the Deity* (2003): "Officium" and "Canticle"; *The Instruments of Art*, (2005): "The Study"; *A Little Book of Hours* (2008): "Slievemore: The Abandoned Village" and "Kane's Lane"; *Eye of the Hare* (2011): "Words of the Unknown Soldier" and "Shoemaker"; *Snow Falling on Chestnut Hill* (2012): "Snow Falling on Chestnut Hill"; *Semibreve,* (2015): "Semibreve", "Viola d'Amore", "Pipe Organ", "Night Prayer", "Pride of Life", "A Birth", "Name and Nature", "Encounter" and "Walls"; *Dear Pilgrims* (2018): "Goldcrest", "Townland" and "According to Lydia"; *Naming of the Bones* (2021): "Aidan: A Life", "Trading Places", "The Gate" and "Omega".

www.carcanet.co.uk

James Harpur: *A Vision of Comets* (1993): "A Vision of Comets"; *The Monk's Dream* (1996): "The Flight of the Sparrow" and "Corn Circle"; *Oracle Bones* (2001): "Magna Karistia", "I Stretch My Arms" and "Cranborne Woods"; *The Dark Age* (2007): "St Symeon Stylites", "Brendan", "Kevin and the Blackbird", and "The Monastic Star-Timetable"; *The Gospel of Joseph of Arimathea* (2008): "*from* Joseph of Arimathea"; *Angels and Harvesters* (2012): "The Falcon Carol", "Finbarr and the Serpent of Gougane Barra", "The Song of Richard Rolle", "Angels and Harvesters" and "The Pram Pusher's Tale"; *The White Silhouette* (2018): "The Perseids", "The White Silhouette", "Verbum" *(from "Kells")*, "Seraphim of Sarov", "The Face" and "Trinity"; *The Oratory of Light* (2021): "Columba's Vision"; Unpublished: "*from* Vacanas" and "The Church of Air".

www.jamesharpur.com